Oregon History

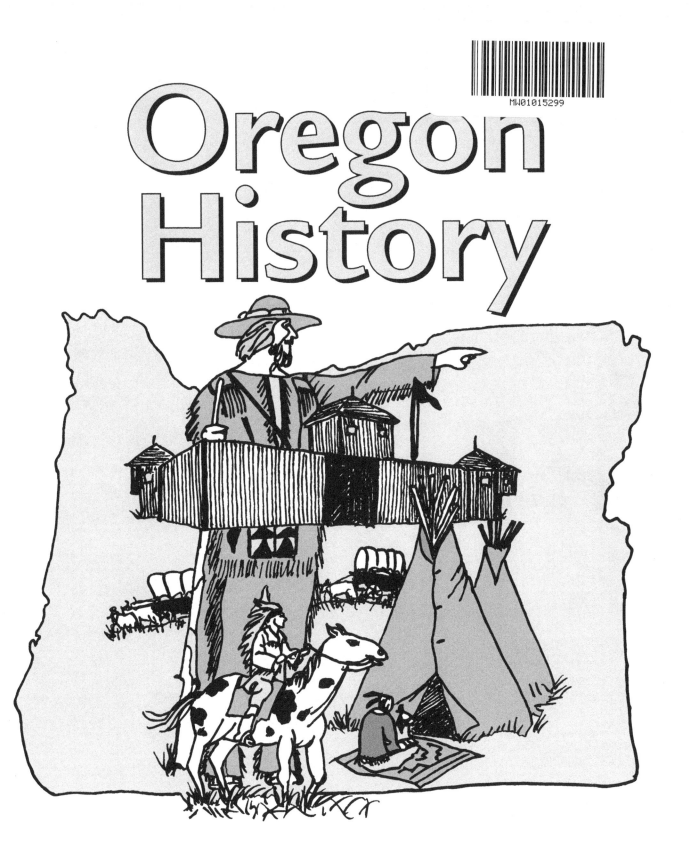

STUDENT WORKBOOK

by Georgia Pennington Sligar

Oregon History

STUDENT WORKBOOK

by Georgia Pennington Sligar

OREGON HISTORY BOOK
Vancouver, Washington
www.oregonhistorybook.com

OREGON HISTORY BOOK

Vancouver, Washington
www.oregonhistorybook.com

© 1985, revised 2000 Georgia Pennington Sligar

ISBN-13: 978-1478230014 • ISBN-10: 1478230010

All Scripture quotations are from the
New King James Version except where noted.

In Appreciation

When writing or compiling a workbook of this type, there are special people who have helped in many creative ways. First of all, praise and honor must go to the Lord Jesus Christ for His saving grace and daily guidance. My thanks to Barbara Wright, former instructor at Portland Bible College, who encouraged me to write this workbook. She then took the time to correct my spelling and grammar. A very special thanks to my friend Marcia Duffel. Marcia spent many long evenings and Saturdays deciphering my handwriting and typing the rough copy. Many thanks to the wives of the Pastors and Elders of City Bible Church (formerly Bible Temple) for their encouragement and prayer support. The administrative staff and teachers of City Christian School, (formerly Bible Temple Christian School), were a daily source of encouragement and strength to me. Bouquets of thanks to you all. Special thanks to Giselle Herem for her proof reading expertise. My heartfelt appreciation to Jim and Laura Davis of C.B.C. for making the second revision, May 2000, a reality.

Lastly, I wish to honor my late husband, Howard (Howdy) B. Sligar, Jr., former Principal of City Christian School, 1978-1991. His confidence in me, prayer support and strength, helped to buoy me up. For the many long miles he drove that I might see, experience and enjoy this wonderful state, Oregon. For the many meals he prepared himself through the writing and re-writing in 1985, I am grateful. Howdy is now with Our Lord Jesus Christ, praising the Lord and walking on the streets of gold. He shall be greatly missed by all who knew him.

Georgia Pennington Sligar
Portland, Oregon 1985
Revised May 2000

Pastor Howard (Howdy) B. Sligar Jr. passed away August 1, 1997.

I will remember the works of the Lord; surely I will remember Your wonders of old. I will also meditate on all Your work.

(Psalm 77:11,12)

Table of Contents

Oregon History Student Workbook

by Georgia Pennington Sligar

Introduction

To complete this workbook, the student will need:

1. A *New King James Version* Bible
2. Dictionary
3. Colored pencils or crayons
4. A road map of the state of Oregon
5. A road map of the state of Washington
6. A computer

Included in each Unit is a list of words for the student to define, using the dictionary. For a special report it would be to the student's benefit, but not necessary, to have a set of encyclopedias. A trip to the library would provide the needed encyclopedias and resource material.

A copy of *The Oregon Bluebook* would also benefit the student. It can be obtained by contacting the office of The Secretary of State in Salem, Oregon, or by calling your local bookstore.

At the end of each unit there is a list of "Suggested Projects" for the student to complete. This may require an adult to supervise, as needed.

This workbook comes complete with eight final tests, a score key and a test key. The eight final tests plus the score key and test key should be kept separate from the student's workbook.

The student is encouraged to color the sketches and fill in the maps with colored pencil or crayon. At the end of this course, when the book is completed, the student may keep this book for reference when traveling around our great state on vacation.

A computer would be helpful for the student. There is a very comprehensive game for a computer with a CD-ROM for Windows and Mac. This game will give the student a real idea of what it was like to travel across the country from Independence, Missouri, to Oregon City, Oregon Territory. Parents and students can play at the same time to see who can get through the entire trip with all their goods, wagon, cattle and people. I highly recommend the game called "The Oregon Trail," which can be purchased at any office supply store.

Some Illustrations

Oregon History

STUDENT WORKBOOK

UNIT I

The Beginning to 1800

- The Beginning
- First People-The Indians
- The Whiteman

STUDENTS' GOAL	
Target Test Date	_____
Pages in Unit	_____
Pages Per Day	_____
Date Unit Completed	_____
Final Score of Unit	_____

UNIT I *The Beginning* to 1800

The Beginning of the World and of Oregon is thought to have begun millions of years ago. Some **secular humanist scientists** have said that the earth started with a "Big Bang." It is their theory that the earth went through many stages of violent geologic and volcanic changes. They call these stages evolution. Liquid granite oozing from the ground caused changes to appear in and on the earth. Great thrusting up and folding of the earth's crust formed the mountains and the valleys.

In your New King James Bible read the entire first chapter of Genesis. Write out verses 1,9,10, in the space below.

Genesis 1:1-31.

Vs.1 _____

_____

_____

_____

Vs.9 _____

_____

_____

_____

Vs. 10 _____

_____

_____

_____

_____

John 1:1,2,3. Write out all three verses in the space below.

Vs.1 _____

_____

_____

Vs.2 _____

_____

Vs.3 _____

_____

_____

_____

Paleontologists tell us that through eons of time, giant fern forests grew in the tropical climate. We are told that huge animals, called dinosaurs, were overwhelmed by lava flows or an unfriendly atmosphere and died in large tar pits. Scientists then tell us that the earth's atmosphere began to cool. Over millions of years the earth entered an ice age, where ice covered the entire earth.

Fossils have been found at high elevations in many mountains around the world. **Geologists** tell us that the fossils of seashells found in these mountains mean that our earth was once covered with water. They say this happened as the ice age ended and the earth started to warm once again.

Genesis 7:1-24. Read these verses then write out verse 19.

_____

_____

_____

_____

_____

_____

_____

God's Word tells us about the earth being covered with water. Today geologists and paleontologists are showing us the fossil seashells they have found at high elevations in the mountains. This clearly shows us that indeed a great flood happened. It was the great flood of Noah.

As the water receded, volcanoes spewed out lava. Many of our mountains were formed as these volcanoes erupted. In the Pacific Northwest, a chain of mountains running from north to south is known as the Cascade Range. Some of the more famous mountains in the Cascade Range are: Mount Baker, Mount Rainier, Mount Hood, Mount Adams, Mount Jefferson, Mount Washington, and Mount Mazama. Mount Mazama is now known as the mountain where you can find Crater Lake. All of these mountains are volcanic.

Using your dictionary, define the following:

1. **extinct** _____

_____

_____

2. **elevation** _____

_____

_____

_____

3. **geology** _____

_____

_____

4. **paleontology** _____

_____

_____

_____

_____

5. **lava** _____

_____

_____

_____

6. **fossil**_____

_____

_____

_____

_____

7. **secular humanist** -(Define this in two parts:

a. secular, b. humanist) **a.** _____

_____

_____

_____

_____

b. _____

_____

_____

_____

_____

_____

8. **eon** _____

_____

_____

_____

9. **atmosphere**_____

_____

_____

_____

_____

10. **volcano** _____

_____

_____

_____

_____

CRATER LAKE

One very significant volcanic action occurred about 8,000 years ago. In southern Oregon Mount Mazama, an active volcano, erupted and spread lava and ashes over hundreds of miles. Today in the deep crater that was once Mount Mazama lies spectacular Crater Lake. Crater Lake is the deepest lake in the United States.

On May 18, 1980, a volcano erupted in our sister state of Washington. The mountain was Mount St. Helens, which is found in southwestern Washington State near the Columbia River. This mountain is also in the Cascade Range.

Today some scientists tell us the approximate age of our earth may be measured by testing its rocks and fossils. They use a carbon-14 test or a radiocarbon test. These tests measure the amount of carbon found in the article which tells the approximate age from within a few years to a few hundred years.

TEST YOUR MEMORY

1. What does Genesis 1:1 say? _____
   _____
   _____

2. The word geology means _____
   _____
   _____
   _____

3. Some secular humanists say that the earth started with
   " _____ ."

4. When a volcano erupts, the hot material that flows out
   is called_____.

5. In Genesis 7, God's Word tells us
   that_____covered the earth
   during Noah's lifetime.

6. Geologists have found _____ at
   high elevations in the mountains.

7. Mount Mazama erupted and today in the deep crater
   lies _____ _____.

8. In what state did the volcano Mount St. Helens erupt? __
   _____

9. The range of mountains that runs north and south is
   called the _____
   _____.

10. Name three mountains in the Cascade Range.
    a. _____
    b. _____
    c. _____

First People

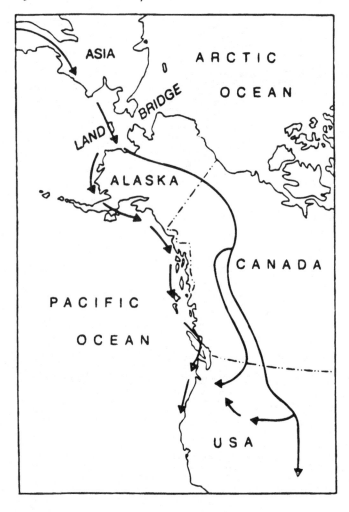

We will call these early people Indians. Today they are called **native Americans**. The Indians of Oregon lived in outlying locations and were isolated from one another. They did not share in the cultural growth of other tribes further east and south. Oregon Indians who lived close to the Pacific Coast had no agriculture and did not work with metals. The only domestic animal they had was the dog. Contact with other tribes was infrequent. The Oregon Indian tribes each had their own distinct language, customs, and tribal laws. Most of the Oregon tribes restricted their movements. They stayed close to home.

The tribes who lived in what is now eastern Oregon were exceptions. As soon as these tribes acquired horses, they traveled as far as the Great Plains to hunt buffalo. The use of horses led the tribes to explore and meet other tribes and expand their culture. There were many tribes of Indians in Oregon in the early days before the white men came to trade for animal skins. We will learn about these white fur trappers a little later. Now let's learn about the Indians of Oregon and the tribes in the Northwest.

FILL IN THE BLANKS:

1. The first people to come to a._____were

   probably from b._____.

2. The only domestic animal they had was the

   _____.

3. The Indian tribes each had their own distinct

   a._____, b._____, and

   c._____ laws.

4. The Indians of yesterday are today

   called_____ _____.

5. The a._____made it possible for the

   Indians to hunt b._____.

The first people to come to the Northwest and the Oregon area were probably from Asia. The route led north and east along the coast of Siberia. Thousands of years ago these people sailed in small boats or walked. About 11,000 B.C. (before Christ) the sea level is thought to have been about 300 feet below the present level. At that time a land bridge at Bering Strait would have made it possible to walk from Asia to the North American continent.

Perhaps the most important route early inhabitants followed led from the Yukon River Valley to the interior plains, then south along the eastern front of the Rocky Mountains, with some people branching off toward the Pacific Coast. Some of them headed toward the Atlantic Coast, while many more settled in Mexico and Central America. They attained a high degree of cultural and social development.

On the map below find three tribes in each group. Underline the name of the tribe with a colored pencil or crayon. Use a different color for each group. (Example: Blue=Coastal Indians; Green=Valley Indians).

The Indians of Oregon can be divided into four (4) groups.

1. Coastal Indians
2. Valley Indians
3. River Indians
4. Plains or Horse Indians

COASTAL INDIANS

PLANK HOUSES
of COAST SALISH

Names of Tribes

Chinook   Siletz
Tillamook   Siuslaw
Clatsop   Coos
Alsea   Salish
Nehalem   Yamhill

Transportation

Dugout canoe
Walking

Clothing

Woven hats, capes and shirts made from plant
    fibers. Capes of lynx and martin skins.
Shirts of seal hair, raccoon or muskrat fur.
Otter skins were used only by "rich"
    Indians.
Capes during the rainy season were often
    made of woven cattail plants and
    cedar fibers.

COASTAL
INDIAN
HAT

Housing

Lodges made of cedar planks.
Several families living together in the same lodge.
Walls of homes lined with skins sewn together.

Diet

Salmon   Clams
Crabs   Seaweed

Small game birds
Deer   Pemmican

VALLEY INDIANS

Names of Tribes

Calapooya*
Molalla
Multnomah
Chinook
Santiam

Transportation

Dugout canoe
Walking

Clothing

Deer hides

Capes and shirts woven from long-leafed plants, fiber and
    tree bark.

Dresses of deer hides were trimmed with seashells.

Blankets made of cloth woven from dog hair, root fibers,
    and deer hides.

Housing

Small lodges of plank wood
covered with cedar bark.

Diet

Salmon   Ducks
Fish   Geese
Deer   Acorns and nuts
Elk   Camas roots
Bear   Wild fruit
Pemmican

*Calapooya has also been recorded as
being spelled Kalapuyas.

RIVER INDIANS

Wickiup of Umatilla Indians

PLAINS OR HORSE INDIANS

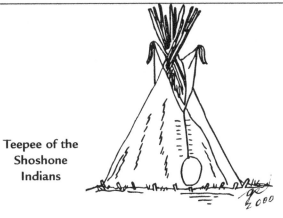

Teepee of the
Shoshone
Indians

Names of Tribes

Columbia   Umatilla
Umpqua   Nez Perce
Rogue   Snake
Klamath Cayuse
Modoc

Transportation

Dugout canoe
Horses
Walking

Clothing

Deer hides
Beaver skins
Rabbit skins
Bearskins

Housing

Haystack-like stick
and grass hut.

Diet

Fish (caught with spears and nets)
Salmon (smoked and dried)
Ducks
Geese
Deer
Pemmican

Names of Tribes

Paiute   Nez Perce
Shoshone   Snake
Bannock
Umatilla

Transportation

Horses
Travois
Walking

Clothing

Buffalo hides
Deer hides
Bear hides
Rabbit skins

Housing

Teepee made from buffalo,
deer and elk hides. Very mobile.
Moved to follow buffalo herds.

Diet

Buffalo   Rabbit
Deer   Bear
Elk   Grouse

These four groups of Indians were very different from each other. The territories of some of the tribes overlapped. They differed in the types of homes they lived in, the food they ate, the way they traveled, and in the clothes they wore.

Oregon Indian Tribes

Listed in Alphabetical Order:

Alsea	Klamath	Shoshone
Bannock	Molalla	Siletz
Calapooya	Modoc	Siuslaw
Cayuse	Multnomah	Snake
Chinook	Nehalem	Tillamook
Clatsop	Nez Perce	Tygh
Columbia	Paiute	Tutuni
Coos	Rogue	Umatilla
Coquille	Salish	Umpqua
Cowlitz	Santiam	Wasco
Deschute		Yamhill

Listed by Groups:

Coastal Indians
Alsea	Siletz
Chinook	Siuslaw
Clatsop	Tillamook
Coos	Salish
Nehalem	Yamhill

Valley Indians
Calapooya	Multnomah
Cowlitz	Santiam
Molalla	

River Indians
Cayuse	Modoc	Snake	Wasco
Columbia	Nez Perce	Umatilla	
Klamath	Rogue	Umpqua	

Plains or Horse Indians
Bannock	Paiute	Snake
Nez Perce	Shoshone	Umatilla

Coastal Indians

The Coastal Indians lived in lodges made from cedar planks. Several families lived in the same lodge. They covered the inside walls with skins of animals sewn together. The families did not move around because it took too long to build their houses.

They stayed by the Pacific Ocean and caught salmon, dug for clams, and caught small game birds for their food. They also ate pemmican. The Indians made pemmican from the meat taken from salmon, birds or deer. The meat would be dried, pounded into a paste, then fat would be added. This mixture would then be formed into cakes. Pemmican was a good source of concentrated high-energy food for the tribes.

Coastal Indians traveled in dugout canoes. They would take a large cedar log and hollow it out by using fire, flint and beaver-toothed chisels.

The clothes they wore were made out of plant fibers that were woven into hats, capes and shirts. They also made clothes from animal skins such as, lynx, martin, raccoon, and muskrat. Only very rich Indians wore capes made of otter skins. In the summer they went barefoot, but in the winter they wore boots made from animal skins for warmth.

Valley Indians

Valley Indians lived in much smaller lodges made of planks covered with cedar bark. Since their houses were smaller they could move around more easily, but they probably did not move often.

They also caught salmon, but they ate more game meat than Coastal Indians, including deer, elk and bear. They ate nuts such as acorns, as well as wild fruit and camas roots.

Valley Indians traveled in dugout canoes that were much smaller and lighter. They were made from birch bark. The frame of the canoe was covered with long strips of birch bark that had been softened in boiling water. These strips were then sewn together to make the outer skin of the canoe.

For clothing the Valley Indians used deer hides and woven plant fibers to make hats, shirts and capes. They wove blankets from dog hair and root fibers.

River Indians

River Indians used the rivers to their best advantage. Their homes were much like the Valley Indians homes but they also built the **wickiup** and the **grass house**. The wickiup was made of tree saplings covered with brush, bark, rush mats or skins. It was made easily and quickly, which allowed them to move about more often.

The grass house was built in a round shape that looked like a haystack. The frame was covered with bundles of grass. These were built quickly and easily.

Like the Valley Indians, River Indians caught fish and salmon. However, River Indians used spears and nets. The salmon was smoked over a small fire and dried for eating later. They also ate ducks, geese, and deer, and made pemmican.

Like the Coastal and Valley Indians, River Indians traveled in dugout, lightweight canoes. They also used horses for travel. They probably traded with the Plains Indians in exchange for the horses.

Most of the River Indians' clothes were made from animal hides. They used hides from deer, beaver and rabbit.

Plains or Horse Indians

The fourth and final group of Indians was the Plains or Horse Indians. They followed the buffalo herds for their meat and hides. Since they were on the move a lot, they needed homes that were easy to build and take down. They also needed an easy way to carry the hides. The Plains Indians lived in a home called a teepee. It was made of long poles put upright in a circle and gathered at the top. Buffalo, deer or elk hides were then placed over the poles. These homes were very easy to put up and take down.

Indians used their horses to travel as well as to move their homes. They made a **travois** of two long poles held together with strips of hide. One end of the pole was tied to one side of a horse while the other pole was tied to the other side of the horse. The ends of the poles dragged on the ground behind the horse. The area between the poles behind the horse was used to haul the family's home and goods.

Plains Indians ate mostly animal meat such as buffalo, deer, elk, rabbit and grouse.

Clothing of hats, capes, and shirts were made from the hides of the animals they killed. Their blankets and robes were made from the treated hides of bears and buffalo. It is said that the Indians used every part of the animal except its voice.

TEST YOUR MEMORY

FILL IN THE FOLLOWING BLANKS.

1. The first people to come to Oregon probably came

   from_____.

2. The Indians were here before the _____ _____

   came to trade.

3. List two (2) Coastal Indian tribes.

   a._____

   b._____

4. List two (2) Valley Indian tribes.

   a._____

   b._____

5. List four (4) River Indian tribes.

   a._____

   b._____

   c._____

   d._____

6. List four (4) Plains Indian tribes.

   a._____

   b._____

   c._____

   d._____

7. What was the type of housing used by:

Coastal Indians _____

Plains Indians _____

8. What type of transportation was used by:

River Indians_____

Plains Indians_____

9. Look up the meaning of the word *travois*. It

means_____

_____

_____

_____

_____.

10. Describe the difference in clothing worn by the

Coastal Indians and the Plains Indians.

_____

_____

_____

_____.

Language Spoken and Written

We will look at the language of only one Indian tribe, the Chinook Indians. **Chinook Jargon** was a trade language spoken by many of the Coastal, Valley and River Indians when they traded with the trappers or the men on large sailing ships.

Chinook jargon was a combination of different languages. Some parts of it were taken from the French fur trappers. Some parts came from words they heard from the English.

You can say that Chinook Jargon was part Chinook, part French, part English, and just plain common sense.

Can you read these phrases? Write them out using the English words.

1. Klootchman Kopa snass_____

_____

2. Tenas klootchman kopa chick-chick _____

_____

Now make up three (3) phrases of your own.

1. _____

_____

2. _____

_____

3. _____

_____

Here is a list of Chinook Jargon and what it means in English

Snass	rain	Tee-hee	laugh
Waum	warm	Kopa	in/toward/from
Cole	cold	wake	no/not
Moos-moos	cow	sun	day
Klootchman	woman	nesika	us/our
Tum-tum	stomach/heart	klaska	them
Tillicum	friend/people	Konawa	all/every
Kaw-kaw	crow	pe	and
Quack-quack	duck	kloshe	good
Tenas moos-moos	little girl	muckamuck	food
Chick-chick	wagon	chickamin	money
Potlatch	give/large feast	tenas	little
Tyee	chief/headman		

Indians of the Pacific Northwest

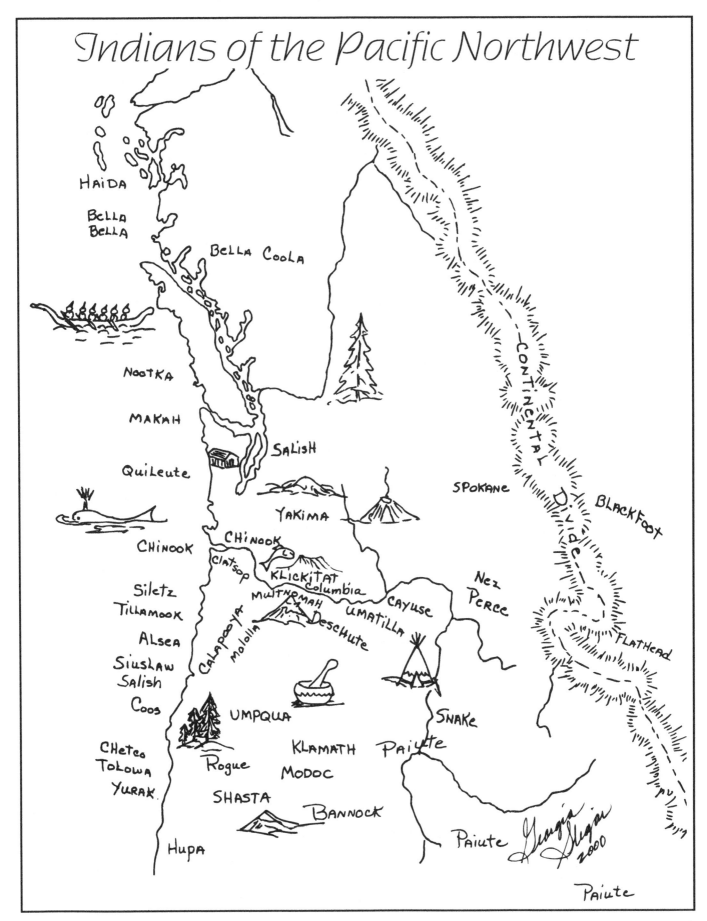

HAIDA

BELLA BELLA

BELLA COOLA

NOOTKA

MAKAH

QUILEUTE

CHINOOK

SALISH

YAKIMA

SPOKANE

BLACKFOOT

CONTINENTAL DIVIDE

CHINOOK

CLATSOP

KLICKITAT

Columbia

NEZ PERCE

FLATHEAD

SILETZ

TILLAMOOK

MULTNOMAH

DESCHUTE

UMATILLA

CAYUSE

ALSEA

SIUSLAW

SALISH

COOS

CALAPOOYA

MOLOLLA

UMPQUA

SNAKE

PAIUTE

CHETCO

TOLOWA

YURAK

ROGUE

KLAMATH

MODOC

SHASTA

BANNOCK

HUPA

PAIUTE   Georgia Hogan 2000

PAIUTE

11

The Lord's Prayer in the Chinook Language

Our	**Father**	**who**	**stayeth**	**in**	**the above**
NESIKA	PAPA	KLAKSTA	MITLITE	KOPA	SAGHALIE
Good	**in**	**our**	**heart**	**(be) thy**	**name;**
KLOSHE	KOPA	NESIKA	TUMTUM	MIKA	NEM;
Good	**thou**	**Chief**	**among**	**all**	**people;**
KLOSHE	MIKA	TYEE	KOPA	KONAWAY	TILLICUM;
Good	**thou**	**will**	**in**	**earth**	
KLOSHE	MIKA	TUMTUM	KOPA	ILLAHIE	
As	**in**	**the above.**			
KAHKWA	KOPA	SAGHALIE.			
Give	**every**	**day**	**our**	**food,**	
POTLATCH	KONAWAY	SUN	NESIKA	MUCKAMUCK,	
If	**we**	**do**	**evil**		
SPOSE	NESIKA	MAMOOK	MASAHCHIE		
Not	**thou**	**very**	**angry**	**and**	**if**
WAKE	MIKA	HYAS	SOLLEKS	PE	SPOSE
Anyone	**evil**	**towards**	**us**		
KLAKSTA	MASAHCHIE	KOPA	NESIKA		
Not	**we**	**angry**	**towards**	**them.**	
WAKE	NESIKA	SOLLEKS	KOPA	KLASKA.	
Send	**away**	**from**	**us**	**all**	**evil**
MAHSH	SIAH	KOPA	NESIKA	KONAWAY	MASAHCHIE.

INDIAN PICTURE SIGNS

In addition to the spoken language, the Indians also drew pictures to tell stories. They had no other written language other than drawing pictures. The pictures would tell a story by using different characters to represent words and deeds. Some tribes drew pictures on deer and buffalo hides that had been treated by the Indian women. This special hide would be handed down from chief to chief. The story on the hide was the history of that particular tribe. One or more pictures would be added each year to tell about the most important thing that had happened to the tribe that year.

THESE ARE SOME OF THE PICTURES THE INDIANS DREW ON THEIR SPECIAL HIDES.

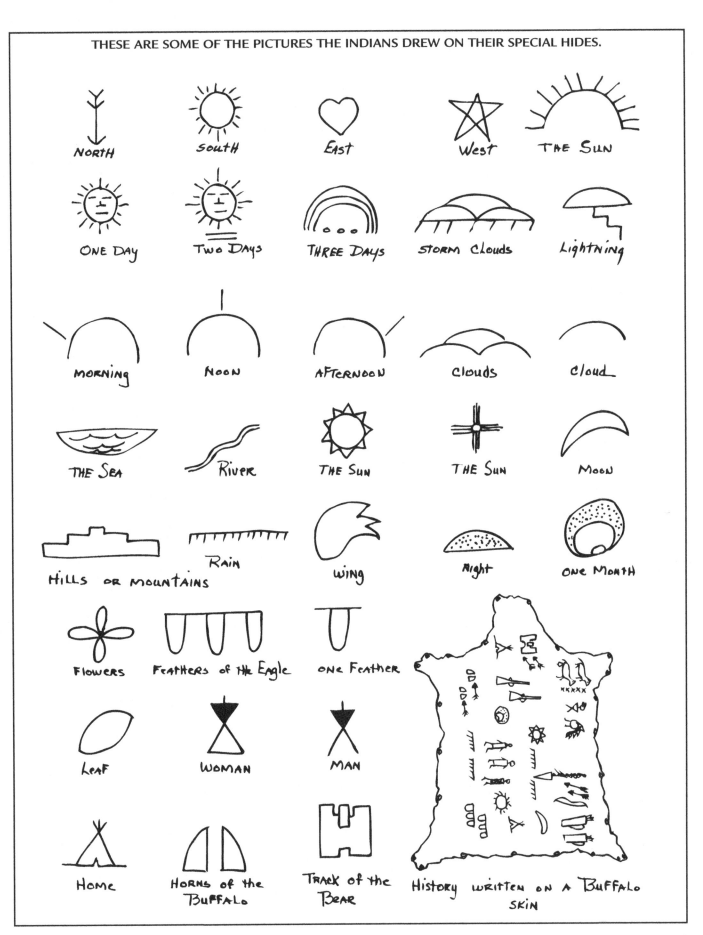

NORTH

SOUTH

EAST

West

THE SUN

ONE DAY

TWO DAYS

THREE DAYS

STORM CLOUDS

Lightning

MORNING

NOON

AFTERNOON

Clouds

Cloud

THE SEA

River

THE SUN

THE SUN

Moon

HILLS OR MOUNTAINS

Rain

WING

Night

ONE MONTH

Flowers

FEATHERS OF THE EAGLE

ONE FEATHER

LEAF

WOMAN

MAN

Home

HORNS of the BUFFALO

Track of the Bear

HISTORY WRITTEN ON A BUFFALO SKIN

WRITE A SHORT PICTURE STORY OF YOUR OWN, USING PICTURE LANGUAGE.

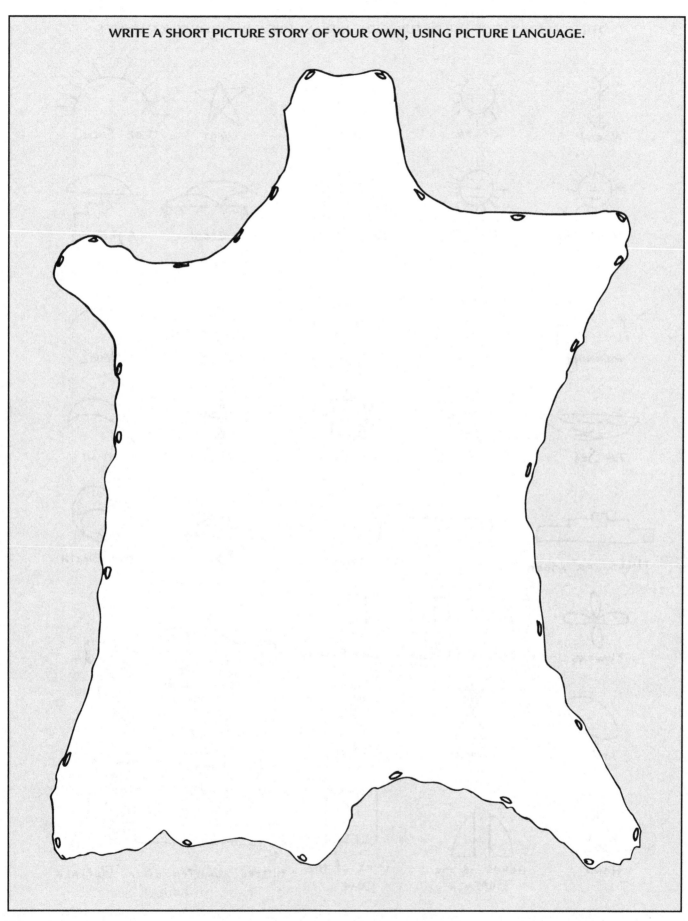

14

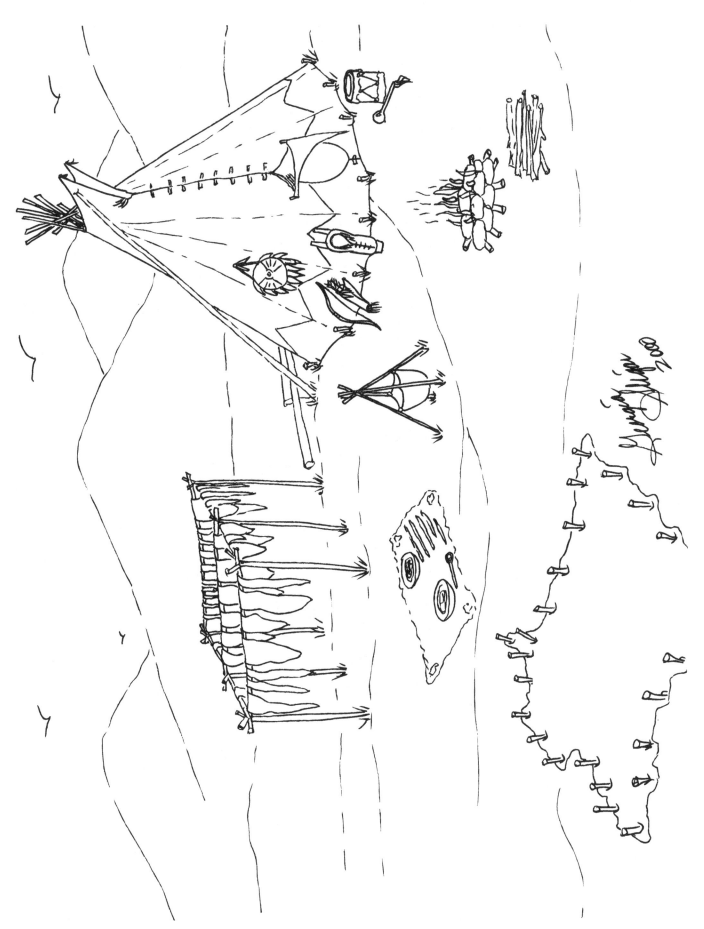

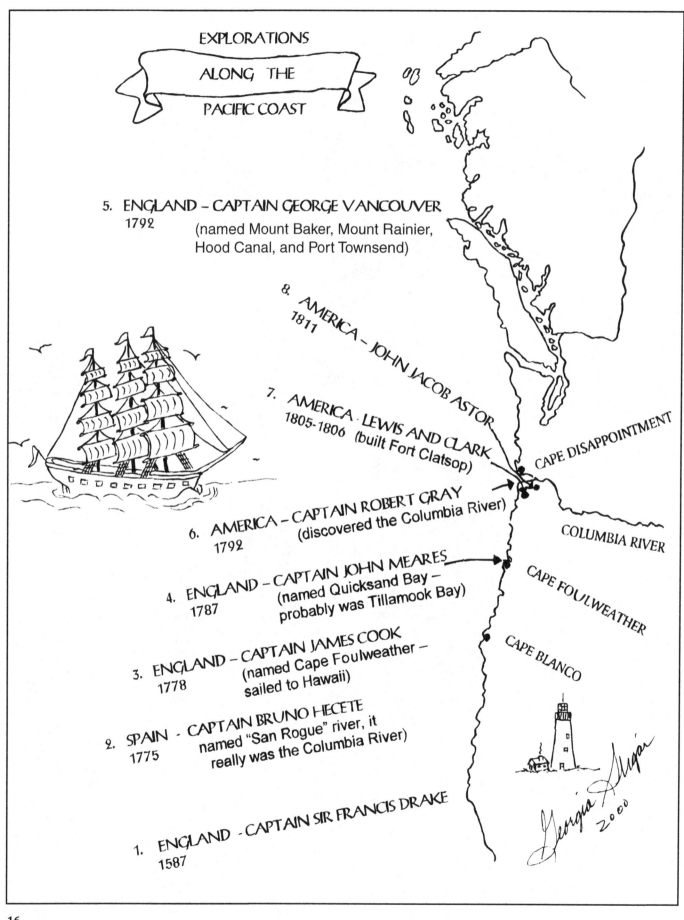

EXPLORATIONS ALONG THE PACIFIC COAST

5. ENGLAND – CAPTAIN GEORGE VANCOUVER
1792
(named Mount Baker, Mount Rainier, Hood Canal, and Port Townsend)

8. AMERICA – JOHN JACOB ASTOR
1811

7. AMERICA - LEWIS AND CLARK
1805-1806 (built Fort Clatsop)

6. AMERICA – CAPTAIN ROBERT GRAY
1792 (discovered the Columbia River)

4. ENGLAND – CAPTAIN JOHN MEARES
1787 (named Quicksand Bay – probably was Tillamook Bay)

3. ENGLAND – CAPTAIN JAMES COOK
1778 (named Cape Foulweather – sailed to Hawaii)

2. SPAIN - CAPTAIN BRUNO HECETE
1775 named "San Rogue" river, it really was the Columbia River)

1. ENGLAND - CAPTAIN SIR FRANCIS DRAKE
1587

CAPE DISAPPOINTMENT

COLUMBIA RIVER

CAPE FOULWEATHER

CAPE BLANCO

Georgia Aligar 2000

The White Man

The white man now enters the story of Oregon. Historians believe that Spanish sailors who sailed from Mexico to the Philippines during the late 1500's and 1600's were the first white men to see the Oregon Coast. Men and women who study history also think that **Sir Francis Drake** of England may have touched Oregon's southern Coast around 1587, when he was searching for an ocean route from the Northern Pacific to the Atlantic Ocean. His ship was named the **Golden Hind.**

In the spring of 1775, the **Spanish** explorer, **Captain Bruno Heceta**, sailed near the Oregon Coast. In his ship's log, he noted a strong current of water emptying into the ocean near latitude north 46° (degrees). He named the river **Rio San Roque**, then sailed south. He stopped long enough off the coast to take depth soundings near the place that is named Heceta Head (north of what is now Florence, Oregon). Captain Heceta then continued south, unable to explore his findings because of the scurvy that plagued his crew. Little did he know that seventeen years later his Rio San Roque would be explored by another and renamed after a ship, the *Columbia*.

There were other famous men who explored and named parts of the Pacific Northwest. **Captain James Cook** was from **England**. He first sighted the Oregon Coast off what is now Yaquina Bay and the city of Newport. He, too, missed the famous river that men were looking for. In 1778, Cape Foulweather was sighted and named by Captain Cook. The Captain then sailed north along the Alaskan coast to where he sighted the Bering Strait. He then turned south to the Sandwich Islands, now called the Hawaiian Islands. In the midst of a quarrel with the natives of the Hawaiian Islands, Captain Cook was killed. Because

Captain Cook was English and had explored parts of the Pacific Northwest, he helped establish a solid claim for the British to the Northwest.

Another English sea captain was **John Meares**. He built a trading post at Nootka Sound where Vancouver Island is now located. **Captain Meares** was a **retired British Naval Officer**. After he retired he sailed for many different countries. He wrote a book, became a successful fur trader, and explored and charted portions of the Northwest coastline. Meares sailed right past the mouth of the *great river* and contradicted Captain Heceta's report by writing that he could safely say that the Rio San Roque did not exist. Captain Meares then sailed farther south to describe and name Quicksand Bay, which is probably what we now call Tillamook Bay.

Still another famous **English** sea captain to miss the great river was **Captain George Vancouver**. He also was instructed to look for a river that might be a passageway for ships from the Pacific to the Atlantic Ocean.

Captain Vancouver named many of the famous places we know today. A few are Admiralty Inlet, Mount Baker, Port Discovery, Mount Rainier, Port Townsend, Port Orchard, Whidbey Island, Hood Canal, Gulf of Georgia and many other places. To claim all this land for England, Captain Vancouver took formal possession of the entire region on June 4, 1792, near the present site of Everett, Washington. He named the region New Georgia, after George III, King of England. Despite all he discovered he still missed the great river.

Next entered the man whose name is very important to Oregon, **Captain Robert Gray**. Captain Gray was a Yankee sailing out of Boston, Massachusetts. He became famous as the **first American** to sail around the world. Captain Gray was sent to the Northwest Coast to trade with the Indians. His orders were to get the furs from the Indians, explore the coastline, then sail to China to trade the furs for goods from China. This was in 1788. Captain Gray got the furs, then traded his ship, the Lady Washington, for a ship named the Columbia Redidiva which was owned by his friend, Captain Kendrick. Now that Captain Robert Gray was on the Columbia Redidiva, he sailed to China. There he traded the furs for goods and returned to Boston by way of the Cape of Good Hope, thus circumnavigating the world.

Define Circumnavigation: _____

_____

_____

_____

In 1791 Captain Gray left Boston for another expedition to the Northwest Coast. He spent the winter of 1791-1792 building the first American sailing ship to be built on the Pacific Coast. He named this ship the Adventure.

In the spring of 1792, Captain Gray began sailing south along the coast in his ship, the Columbia. He wanted to trade again with the Indians. After sailing by the coastline of southern Oregon, he turned and began sailing north, looking for a safe and sheltered anchorage for his ship. He sighted what looked like a wide-mouthed river, but the seas were so heavy, he was unable to get close. He continued up the coast and discovered a safe harbor. The harbor on the Washington coast is named after him, and is called Gray's Harbor to this day.

After a short time the seas calmed and Captain Gray decided to sail south again to look for that wide-mouthed river. This time he sent a small boat to locate a safe channel across the sandbar at the mouth of the river. The small boat showed the way for the large ship, the *Columbia*.

According to the ship's log, the river was sighted on May 11, 1792 at 4 A.M. The Columbia crossed the sandbar at 8 A.M. and by 1 P.M. the ship was anchored in a pleasant sandy cove.

Captain Robert Gray named the Columbia River after his ship. He then named the cape to the south, Adams, and the one to the north, Hancock. Today Cape Hancock is called Cape Disappointment.

For the United States, the discovery of the Columbia River by an American was very important. The United States, a young country with plenty of room to expand overland from the east to the west, had not participated in the naval explorations on the Northwest Coast. Now the United States, as well as England and Spain, held a claim by right of discovery and exploration.

One chief reason the Pacific Northwest was important to the white man was due to an animal called the beaver. The fur trade began growing as more and more men wanted to get rich from trapping, trading and selling beaver skins. We will study the beaver trapper shortly.

UNIT I

Test Your Memory

MATCHING

a. Asia
g. Coastal

b. Seashells
h. Washington

c. Big Bang
i Horse

d. Radiocarbon or Carbon 14

e. Lava
j Cascade Range

f. Crater Lake

1. _____ Some secular humanist scientists say the earth started with a?

2. _____ The hot material that flows out of a volcano is called?

3. _____ What fossils have been found high up on some mountains?

4. _____ Mount Mazama erupted and today we find what, in its deep crater?

5. _____ The name of the mountain range that runs north and south?

6. _____ The first people to come to the Oregon area probably came from?

7. _____ In what state did the eruption of Mount St. Helens take place?

8. _____ A special test tells us the approximate age of plants or animals?

9. _____ Indians living near the Pacific Ocean were called?

10. _____ What animal made it easier for the Indians to travel?

TRUE OR FALSE

11. _____ Historians believe that the English were the first white men to see the Oregon Coast.

12. _____ The Columbia River was named after Captain James Cook's ship.

13. _____ Captain John Meares built a trading post at Nootka Sound.

14. _____ Captain Robert Gray found the Columbia River.

15. _____ Captain George Vancouver named many places like Mount Baker and Mount Rainier.

FILL IN THE BLANKS

16. List the names of the five ships' captains who explored the Pacific Northwest coastline since Sir Francis Drake in 1587.

a. _____

b. _____

c. _____

d. _____

e. _____

17. What does Genesis 1:1 tell us _____

_____

_____.

18. Name the four Indian groups in Oregon.

a. _____ c. _____

b. _____ d. _____

NOW GO BACK AND STUDY ALL THE QUESTIONS FOR UNIT I TO PREPARE FOR THE FINAL TEST.

Suggested Projects

1. Draw a picture of a giant forest.

2. Draw a picture of an erupting volcano.

3. Make a clay (or flour and water) model of a volcano.

4. Get a road map of the states of Oregon and Washington. Find and circle all the mountains you learned about.

5. On your map color Mount St. Helens red.

6. Visit the Interpretive Center at Mount St. Helens. Check the directions on your map.

7. Build a model of an Indian dwelling or village from one of the four groups listed.

8. Using twigs, make your own travois.

9. Build your own dugout canoe out of balsa wood.

10. Find a world map. Mark all the places these captains came from and where they travelled.

Oregon History

S T U D E N T   W O R K B O O K

UNIT II
Exploration Westward and Mountain Men 1801 — 1830

· Lewis and Clark
· Fur Trappers
· Joint Occupation

STUDENTS' GOAL	
Target Test Date	_____
Pages in Unit	_____
Pages Per Day	_____
Date Unit Completed	_____
Final Score of Unit	_____

UNIT II

Exploration Westward and Mountain Men 1801—1830

In the year **1803**, the President of the United States was **Thomas Jefferson**. President Jefferson had long been interested in what lay westward beyond the Mississippi River. When the ruler of France, **Napoleon Bonaparte**, offered to sell not only New Orleans but also all of Louisiana to the United States, President Jefferson agreed to the purchase.

In 1803 the United States of America bought the land from France, calling it the **Louisiana Purchase**. The land bordered the Mississippi River from New Orleans north into what is now the state of Minnesota and west into the Rocky Mountains.

Thomas Jefferson

1783 - Original 13 colonies and territory acquired from Great Britain

President Jefferson hoped to discover more about the land just purchased and perhaps find out more about the country further to the west. There were three reasons for exploring the new land. **First**, the men that went hoped to find a water passage from the Missouri River to the Pacific Ocean. **Secondly**, Jefferson was aware of the great wealth of the fur trade, and he wanted the United States to share in it. **Thirdly**, the explorers would also gather important information about the climate, topography, vegetation, animal life, and Indian tribes.

The president selected his personal secretary, **Meriwether Lewis**, to head the expedition. Lewis had served in the army on the frontier. He knew the way of the Indians and wildlife. Meriwether Lewis was well educated and ready to take the job.

Lewis asked that **William Clark** be named as co-leader. Clark was also

Meriwether Lewis   **William Clark**

an army man with even more experience on the frontier than Lewis. Lewis and Clark, as a team, gathered men and supplies for the adventure west.

The expedition officially became known as the **Corps of Volunteers for the Northwest Discovery**. Later the name was shortened to **Corps of Discovery**. Today, everyone remembers the expedition as the **Lewis and Clark expedition**. The expedition included United States Army regulars, backwoodsmen, hunters, and boatmen.

For You are my rock and my fortress; therefore, for Your name's sake, lead me and guide me (Psalm 31:3).

21

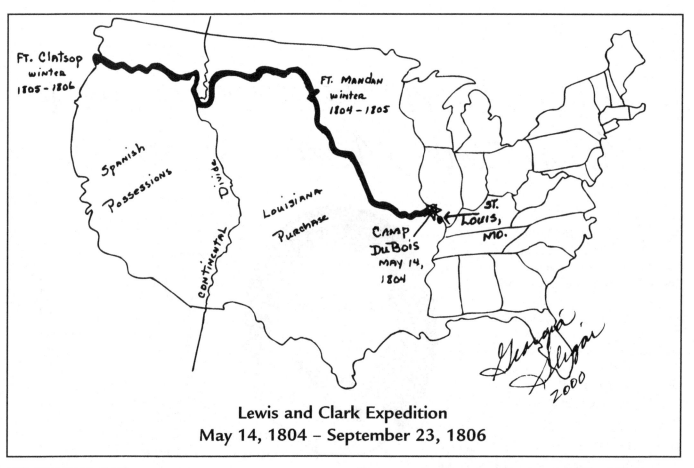

Lewis and Clark Expedition
May 14, 1804 – September 23, 1806

Map labels: Ft. Clatsop winter 1805–1806; Ft. Mandan winter 1804–1805; Spanish Possessions; Continental Divide; Louisiana Purchase; St. Louis, Mo.; Camp DuBois May 14, 1804; Georgia Glynn 2000

FILL IN THE BLANKS:

1. In 1803 the President of the United States was

   _____ _____ .

2. The land that the United States bought from France

   was called the _____ .

3. The ruler of France at that time was _____

   _____ .

4. The names of the two men chosen to lead the expedition

   were:

   a. Meriwether _____

   b. William _____ .

5. What was the shortened name of the expedition?

   _____

   _____

The party of perhaps **forty-five men left Wood River, Illinois, on May 14, 1804**. There were thirty men that were assigned permanently, ten French men were hired to help carry stores and repel any Indian attack. In addition six soldiers were assigned as escorts. The soldiers, like the Frenchmen, were to travel only as far as the first winter encampment. Clark led the men toward St. Charles and Lewis would catch up with the expedition, riding overland from St. Louis. With Lewis and Clark, the group of men leaving **Camp DuBois**, at the mouth of the **Wood River**, totaled **forty-five**. This party of men journeyed into the little known Missouri River country.

During the journey, Lewis would often walk along the riverbank drawing pictures of every animal and new type of tree, bush, or flower he would see. He also drew maps of the area and sometimes named rivers, creeks, and hills. William Clark stayed with the men and boats. (For the entire story of the Lewis and Clark trip, read *The Journals of Lewis and Clark,* a new selection with an introduction by John Bakeless).

The expedition traveled by flat-bottomed boats called **pirogues**. They traveled up the Missouri River to a **Mandan Indian village** in what is now North Dakota. The party of explorers knew that winter was upon them. They could go no further because of the harsh weather. They stayed with the Mandan tribe the winter of 1804-1805. There at the

22

Mandan Indian village a **French Canadian** fur trapper and interpreter by the name of **Toussaint Charbonneau** and his Indian wife, **Sacagawea**, met Lewis and Clark.

Sacagawea had been kidnapped some years earlier. She was taken from her Shoshone Indian tribe family by a warring tribe of **Minnetaree Indians**. Charbonneau had bought her from the Minnetarees. When Charbonneau heard that these men, Lewis and Clark, were going west, he offered to go along and take his wife. He explained that she was a **Shoshone** and could help the expedition. She would be able to help guide them over the rough terrain.

When the Corps of Discovery ran out of water and could no longer use their boats, the pirogues, Sacagawea could help. They would need **horses** to get over the mountains and the Shoshone people were known as **horse Indians**. Sacagawea could get her people to help Lewis and Clark by getting them the horses they would need. Lewis and Clark felt that Sacagawea would be a great asset to the expedition.

Sacagawea's name meant "**bird woman**," but Lewis and Clark gave her the nickname of **Janey**. She was about to become a mother. The baby was due to be born in early February. Lewis and Clark consulted an old French-Canadian trader who had lived with the Indians for 15 years. The trader said that to help Sacagawea during the birth, she should be given a small portion of powdered rattlesnake's rattle. They found a discarded rattle and crushed two small rings, mixed the powder with water, and gave it to Sacagawea to drink. In a very short time she gave birth to a beautiful baby boy. His father, Charbonneau, named the baby **Jean Baptiste** but Lewis and Clark called him **Pompii**.

There was only one **black man** on the expedition. The servant of William Clark, his name was **York**. York was the subject of many curious Indian investigations. Many of the Indian nations would paint parts of their bodies black and other colors in preparation for war with enemy Indian tribes. They could not believe that this man had been born this way and had not painted his body black.

York had to submit himself for their inspection. He would stand in the center of their huts, surrounded by the tribal chiefs and the lesser chiefs. The Indians would then spit on their fingers and try to rub the black off of York's chest, back and arms. Poor York! He was a very patient man, and he knew that it was important to the success of the expedition that he not offend the Indians. Many, many times during the trip, York had to submit to the "**wet finger, rubbing test**."

Mandan earth lodge

FILL IN THE BLANKS:

1. The flat-bottomed boats were called _____.

2. Lewis and Clark spent the first winter with the

_____ Indians.

3. Name the Indian who joined the expedition

_____.

4. She was from what Indian tribe? _____.

5. She had been captured by what Indian

tribe?_____

6. Lewis and Clark crushed _____

and mixed it with water for Sacagawea to drink.

7. Sacagawea's nickname was_____.

8. Lewis and Clark called the baby_____.

9. _____was the only black man with the

expedition.

10. York submitted himself to the

"_____ _____

_____" test.

Leaving the Mandan Indian village in early **April 1805,** the Corps of Discovery now numbering twenty nine, pushed on toward the **Rocky Mountains.** They still needed horses. They wondered if they would meet the Shoshones and if the Indians would remember the young woman who was with them. If the Indians remembered Sacagawea, would they then sell horses to the men of the expedition? All these questions were uppermost in their minds as they left the Mandan Indian village.

As they traveled west, they had the two pirogues and six new dugout canoes that they had built during the winter with the Mandans. They ventured through prairies and low, rolling hills. They saw large herds of **buffalo, elk** and **antelope.** Soon after leaving the Mandan village they had their first serious encounter with **grizzly bears.** On several occasions the men had to leave the land and run into the water or streams to save themselves from the grizzly bears. Once, even the faithful **Scannon,** a large black Newfoundland dog belonging to Lewis, helped chase a bear away from the camp. In some books the faithful Scannon is called Scammon and in others, Seaman. We shall call him Scannon.

The expedition was now coming into Shoshone country. It was mid-August and the men knew they had to have horses soon. They had to get over the Rocky Mountains before the harsh winter set in. The Indians called the mountains, the **Shining Mountains.**

The men finally sighted Indians on horseback but when they tried to get close, the Indians would ride away. One day Lewis came around a small hill and found an old woman, a younger woman, and a little girl. Lewis gave them small

presents and then put vermillion-colored paint on the cheeks of the women as a sign of peace. The women and Lewis had walked about two miles when 60 warriors on horseback came riding up to meet them. The women explained to the warriors that the white men were friends. Lewis further showed that he was a friend by spreading a blanket on the ground as a sign of peace and gave the warriors presents.

Before Lewis and Clark left for the west, they added special presents that they hoped the Indians would like. They brought blue beads, calico shirts, handkerchiefs, needles, thimbles, ribbons, sheet metal, kettles, brass rings to be worn on the fingers, some moccasin awls, several strands of different colored beads, some vermilion paint and some looking glasses or mirrors. The vermilion paint was a bright red to reddish-orange color. President Jefferson also had some peace medals made to give to the Indians. These medals had the profile of President Jefferson on one side and two hands clasped in friendship on the other side. All of these gifts were to be given to the Indian chiefs as a sign of friendship from their white brothers.

FILL IN THE BLANKS:

1. The large bear the men ran from was a

   _____ bear.

2. _____ was the name of Lewis's

   dog.

3. The Indians called the Rocky Mountains the

   _____ _____.

4. The men needed _____ to get

   over the mountains.

5. A sign of peace was spreading a _____

   on the ground.

The Indian chief standing before them was the Shoshone Indian Chief, **Cameahwait.** He was friendly to Lewis and showed him, by sign language, that they should rest and gather in a large circle and smoke a pipe of peace.

As they rested Lewis explained their mission and desire to cross the **Shining Mountains** and the great need for horses to get over the mountains.

On August 17, 1805, as Lewis was bringing Chief Cameahwait back to the expedition camp to meet

Clark, they saw Sacagawea ahead of Clark. She recognized the Indian chief as her long-lost brother. She ran to him, threw her blanket around his shoulders and wept. It was a grand reunion. Cameahwait knew this was his little sister, who had been taken captive by the Minnetaree Indian tribe years before. Sacagawea had found her family again. She interpreted for Lewis and Clark and told her brother what the white men needed. She was also able to tell her brother just how these white men had helped her and her husband and new baby son. Now her brother wanted to help these white men, who had helped his little sister. He was glad to help provide them with horses, as many as they would need.

After resting for a short time, the expedition set off on horseback, leaving the canoes behind. Sacagawea wanted to remain with Lewis and Clark until they reached the great sea. The great sea was what the white men called the Pacific Ocean. She bid her brother and her people good-by and continued westward.

The journey continued. They had great hardships but they finally crossed the **Shining Mountains**. They had to fight their way through blizzards and snowdrifts. It was the month of October and winter was beginning to set in.

The men pushed on. They made it! They were across and going down the other side of the Rocky Mountains. They had crossed the **Continental Divide**. Now all the streams, creeks, and rivers flowed west toward the Pacific Ocean. The expedition met many different Indian tribes along the way. One friendly tribe was the **Nez Perce Indians**. The Nez Perce chief agreed to keep the horses until Lewis and Clark returned for them. Here at the Clearwater River they again built canoes for the rest of the journey to the Pacific Ocean.

FILL IN THE BLANKS:

1. The Shoshone Indian chief's name was _____

_____.

2. The chief was a _____ to Sacagawea.

3. The expedition crossed the

_____ _____

and now all the streams, creeks, and rivers flowed

_____.

Using your dictionary, define the following:

4. topography _____

_____

_____

_____

_____.

5. pirogues _____

_____

_____

_____.

6. portage _____

_____

_____

_____.

7. pelt _____

_____

_____

_____.

8. rendezvous _____

_____

_____

_____.

9. bastion _____

_____

_____

_____.

10. evaporation _____

_____

_____

_____.

There were many dangers, waterfalls, unknown rivers, and white-water rapids. There were times when the canoes overturned in the rapids. Other times the men were forced to portage around the more treacherous parts of the rivers.

Lewis and Clark finally arrived at the mouth of the **Columbia River** and made camp at **Baker's Bay, on the north shore**, just inside what we now call the **Cape Disappointment** area. What a sight they saw. The ocean was so grand and beautiful. They had done it! They had traveled across uncharted land, struggled over rivers, mountains, met hostile and friendly Indians, by-passed savage animals, and suffered untold dangers. Yes, they had arrived at the Pacific Ocean. **They had found an overland route from the east to the west.** Still there was much work to be done. They could not rest, not yet. The date was **November 7th, 1805**, but before they could celebrate there was much to do, to study, to record, and much to get done before the return trip.

The expedition hoped they could return east, at least as far as the Fort Mandan village before the winter set in. Cold weather was upon them and they knew it was too late to get back across the Rocky Mountains. They would have to spend the winter on the Pacific Coast.

Plans had to be made. Lewis and Clark conferred with some of the local Indians and decided to build a fortress on the south side of the Columbia River. The winter of 1805-1806 was a busy one. They would have to build a shelter for the people of the expedition. There were Lewis,

Clark, the men of the Corps of Discovery, Charbonneau, Sacagawea, the baby Pompii, York and the famous dog, Scannon. They all needed to repair the clothes they wore and make new clothes. The canoes were in need of repair and they needed **salt**. Yes, salt. Salt was a necessary staple for life. Men needed salt, not only for themselves and their general health, but also to help preserve game meat.

The men started out immediately to do all that had to be done. Lewis sent several men to the ocean beaches to build fires. Large kettles were filled with ocean salt water, then set on the fires. The water was boiled until it evaporated. What remained in the large kettles was course, sea salt.

Men were put to work building the fort, while others were sent out to get food. The fort was finally ready and they moved into their new winter quarters on the **23rd of December, 1805**. The men named their new winter quarters, **Fort Clatsop**, after the Clatsop Indian tribe. The men of the expedition, the Shoshone woman, her French-Canadian husband, the baby, the black man, and the dog, all enjoyed a quiet Christmas Day. The next few months were spent getting ready for the return trip to St. Louis and the civilized United States.

1805-1806
Fort Clatsop

ConstaL
Indian
Hat

**Drawings from the Journals of
Lewis and Clark**

Head flattening
Lower Columbia

On their journey west, Lewis and Clark had made drawings of plants, animals and trees that they were not familiar with. They also made maps of rivers, creeks, and streams with painstaking accuracy. During the winter at Fort Clatsop they put their drawings, maps and journals in order. They would need to report to President Jefferson, what they had found and all the new information about this new country they had explored.

On **March 23, 1806**, the men packed their canoes with their few belongings and said goodbye to Fort Clatsop and the Pacific Ocean. The Corps of Discovery started back up the Columbia River, over the mountains, toward home.

The expedition was very important for the United States. The explorers had traveled more than 4,000 miles. They had faced the hazards of unknown trails. So many treacherous rivers and snow-covered mountain ranges had to be crossed. They had suffered attacks by large animals and hostile Indian tribes but had also met many friendly Indian tribes. Only one man, Sergeant Floyd, was lost during this whole trip. This man died from an illness shortly after the journey began.

The expedition was a great success. Having explored the area drained by the Columbia River and built Fort Clatsop, they had strengthened America's claim on this new territory to become part of the United States. The Corps of Discovery proved the existence of a tremendous mountain range between the headwaters of the Missouri River and the Pacific Ocean.

The journals written by Meriwether Lewis, William Clark, and the others provided details about the physical characteristics of the region, plant and animal life, topography and climate. Not the least of which was the information

about the Indian tribes in the Northwest. All the drawings and sketches in the journals would be invaluable. In addition, they established friendly relations with some of the Indian tribes. All in all, the trip was very successful.

FILL IN THE BLANKS:

1. Lewis and Clark arrived at the Pacific Ocean in the

   month of _____.

2. The building for their winter quarters was named

   _____ _____.

3. The men and Sacagawea moved into the fort two days

   before _____.

4. The expedition left for home in the month of

   _____.

5. More than _____ miles had been traveled.

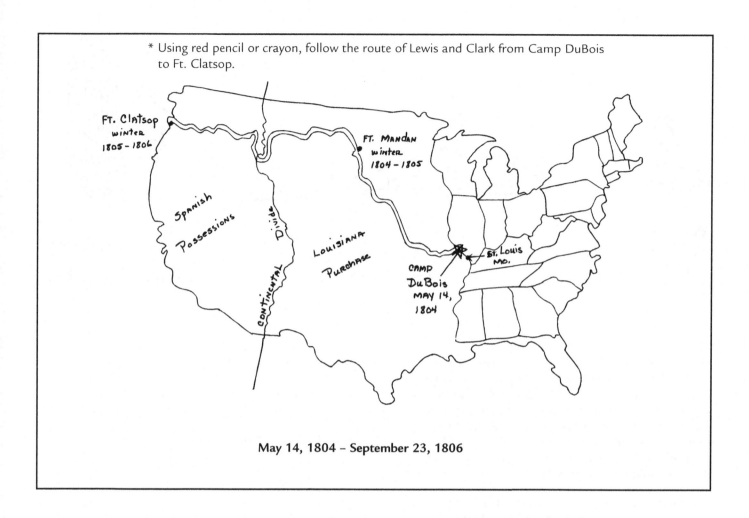

* Using red pencil or crayon, follow the route of Lewis and Clark from Camp DuBois to Ft. Clatsop.

FT. Clatsop winter 1805-1806

FT. Mandan winter 1804-1805

Spanish Possessions

Continental Divide

Louisiana Purchase

St. Louis MO.

CAMP DuBois MAY 14, 1804

May 14, 1804 – September 23, 1806

Timeline, dates, places of the Lewis and Clark expedition

May	14	1804	Left Wood River.
August	1	1804	Powwow with Chiefs of Poncas, Omahas, Otos at Council Bluffs.
August	20	1804	Sgt. Charles Floyd died, only death on trip.
Sept.	25	1804	Expedition defied Teton Sioux, pushed upriver.
Oct.	10	1804	Reached Arikara Village.
WINTER OF 1804-1805			FORT MANDAN BUILT, SPENT WINTER.
April	7	1805	Expedition resumed trek west.
June	21-		
July	15	1805	Portaged 17 miles around Great Falls.
July	15	1805	Reached three forks of Missouri River.
Aug.	12	1805	Lemhi Pass, first white men to cross the Continental Divide in this part of North America.

Aug.	17	1805	Traded for horses at Shoshone Village, Sacagawea met her brother, the chief.
Oct.	25	1805	Portaged Columbia River rapids at The Dalles.
Nov.	7	1805	Arrived at the Pacific Ocean.
WINTER OF 1805-1806			FORT CLATSOP BUILT, SPENT WINTER.
Mar.	23	1806	Started back east.
July	3	1806	Travelers rested, expedition divided.
July	27	1806	Exploring Maria's River, Lewis and 3 men fought Blackfoot Indians.
Aug.	11	1806	Lewis accidentally shot.
Aug.	12	1806	Lewis met Dickson and Hancock, first of the mountain men, Lewis joined Clark.
Sept.	23	1806	The CORPS OF DISCOVERY RETURNED TO ST. LOUIS, MISSOURI.

Mountain Men and Fur Trappers

The "mountain man" was a different kind of man. To understand what made men leave their families, friends, trades, and businesses, we need to find out what drew them to the harsh Northwest mountains. The answer, though it is simple, seems complex. They felt the need to be free, to be alone, to find out **what was over the next hill**, and what adventures they would have the next day.

These men were adventurers. They needed to prove to themselves and others that they could survive, with God's help, and with their own resourcefulness.

Trust in the Lord with all your heart, and lean not on your own understanding; in all your ways acknowledge Him, and He shall direct your paths (Proverbs 3:5,6).

There was another reason, **money!** Some men hoped to become rich in a short time by working in the **fur trade**. Some did get rich, rich for themselves or by hiring others to work for them. Others failed and some even died, in spite of all their efforts.

The much-sought after **mountain beaver** was the most important reason they traveled so far north and west. An adult mountain beaver could weigh as much as **60 pounds**. Aside from his long front teeth, his flat tail, his skill at building a dam or his staying with a single mate, there's little about him that's unusual, that is except for

one thing, his thick underfur. Called **muffoon**, this thick underfur was minutely barbed, making it unmatched for the making of felt.

For a couple of centuries, from around 1600 well into the 1800s, few gentlemen, on either side of the Atlantic, would leave the house without wearing their **beaver felt hats**. In the early 1800s the **ladies also wanted their hats to be made of beaver felt**. In addition, the ladies liked their robes, shawls, capes and hand-held muffs to be trimmed with the fur of the beaver.

This small animal and the whim of fashion opened the Northwest to the mountain men and the fur companies and wealth.

FILL IN THE BLANKS:

1. Mountain men wanted to know what was over the next

   _____.

2. An adult mountain beaver could weigh up to

   _____.

3. The thick underfur is called _____.

4. The underfur was made into _____ hats for men.

5. In the early 1800s _____ also wanted their

   hats to be made from felt.

The companies who did business in the Rocky Mountains also entered the Oregon Territory. The first such company to set up an official trading post was the **Pacific Fur Company, founded by John Jacob Astor**. His fur company traded goods and supplies to the trappers in exchange for the beaver pelts they had trapped, cleaned and cured.

Astor wanted to build a trading post on the Columbia River. He sent out two different parties, each with orders to establish a post on the Columbia. **The first party** left New York and sailed aboard the ship, **Tonquin**. Captain

Jonathan Thorn was the captain of the Tonquin. **The second party** set out from St. Louis on an overland expedition to the mouth of the Columbia, similar to the one led by Lewis and Clark. **Wilson Price Hunt** led the second party. Astor also sent a second ship, the Beaver, with a load of supplies and men.

There was much grief aboard the Tonquin. Captain Thorn was an unreasonable man, and by the time they arrived at the mouth of the Columbia River there were many hard feelings. Captain Thorn sent a small boat to cross the sandbar at the mouth of the Columbia River. The weather was stormy and the crossing was treacherous. Instead of waiting for more favorable weather, Thorn insisted the small boat go out. The small boat and the crew of five men were crushed and killed by the huge breakers. A few days later Captain Thorn sent out another small boat whose three-man crew was also lost.

The Tonquin finally crossed the bar but with the loss of eight men. The men of the Pacific Fur Company left the ship and selected a site for the trading post to be built.

Eager to begin trading with the Indians, Captain Thorn left the Columbia River area and sailed north to **Vancouver Island**. While there, he antagonized the Indians, a fight broke out, and all but one man aboard the Tonquin was killed. The next day that man enticed the Indians back on board the ship. While the Indians were on the upper decks of the ship, this man went into the hold, below decks, and set the powder magazine on fire. There was a huge explosion, killing all the Indians on board the ship including the one white man. The blast totally demolished the Tonquin.

When the men waiting at the mouth of the Columbia River received word about the loss of the Tonquin and all their supplies, they were saddened. The men made the most of their predicament. They continued to build a trading post, naming it **Fort Astoria** after John Jacob Astor. They began trading with the Indians with their remaining supplies. Some of the men went further up the Columbia to establish another trading post.

The overland party of the Pacific Fur Company, led by Wilson Price Hunt, also suffered many hardships. They fought hostile Indians, experienced sickness, starvation and fatigue. Some of the men even deserted. When they finally reached Astoria in 1812, 17 months after leaving St. Louis, only 35 out of 59 men remained.

FILL IN THE BLANKS:

1. John _____ _____

founded the Pacific Fur Company.

2. The ship _____

sailed to the Columbia River.

3. Another party of men went _____.

4. What destroyed the ship Tonquin?

_____

_____.

5. The name of the trading post was _____

_____.

In May of 1812 the supply ship Beaver arrived at Astoria. The spirits of the men lifted. They now had supplies to trade with the Indians for the much-sought after beaver pelts. The furs the men gathered were sent by ship to China and traded for Chinese goods, which were then shipped back to New York.

The Pacific Fur Company was the first company to have a post on the Pacific Coast to carry on a trading operation. There was another company that had to be reckoned with, and that was the North West Company, owned by the British. Its headquarters was in Montreal, Canada.

The year was now **1812** and the **United States was at war with Great Britain**. When word reached the men that there was war, a very uneasy winter was spent at Astoria.

The North West Company, called Nor'westers, had set up a camp outside Fort Astoria. They warned the Astorians that a British warship would soon arrive and seize the fort. It would be wise, they argued, to sell the fort while there was still time, rather than risk losing everything and being killed. The Astorians, not having had any orders from John Jacob Astor, finally gave in and sold the fort.

The British took over **Fort Astoria** and changed the name to **Fort George**. Now the Nor'westers had a headquarters for their western trading. For eight years, from 1813 to 1821, they had no competition in the Northwest.

The men who went out to trap the beaver believed they could do a better job than the Indians. So the fur companies sent out white men for a year to gather the pelts. The trapper went to any area that had several clear streams and beaver dams. The trapping began in early fall, tapering off as winter set in and the streams iced over and deep snow made travel and trapping impossible. Then in the spring the trapping resumed after the spring thaw.

Trapping required considerable skill and know-how, especially about the ways of "Mr. Beaver." After finding an active pond or dam, the traps were set carefully and then scented to attract the animals. The traps were then placed under water. Gum camphor, cinnamon, cloves and juniper oil all made good lures. The most effective lure, called castoreum, was a pungent glandular musk from the beaver himself.

The traps were made of steel, had twin springs and weighed about five pounds each. The cost was $14.00 for each trap. The trappers carried about a half dozen traps. These traps were set in such a way that the beaver caught his paw in the trap that was placed under the water. He would drown trying to get loose.

Once a year all the trappers got together at a pre-planned place for what they called the **rendezvous**. This meeting was an important part of the trapper's life. One of the biggest mountain men meetings was held at the **Green River rendezvous**. All year, from fall to summer he was busy trapping and curing the beaver pelts. The rendezvous was a time to turn in, or trade, his hard-earned pelts. With the pelts he could either pay off last year's debt or barter for this year's supplies. They would have to last him until the next year at Rendezvous time.

Some of the supplies he would need included: new traps, salt, flour, coffee, tea, tobacco, gunpowder, lead, a knife, a new bullet mold, and maybe a new rifle. He would have two horses, one for riding and one to carry his supplies. Sometimes he had two mules that were more surefooted than horses.

The rendezvous was a special time to renew old friendships, tell of adventures they'd had, and swap a few tall tales. The Green River rendezvous saw some of the most famous mountain men such as Jim Bridger, Thomas Fitzpatrick, Jedediah Smith, Bill Sublette, Milton Sublette, Hugh Glass, and the famous **Joe Meek**. We will learn more about Joe Meek and his part in Oregon history later in this workbook.

The Indian tribes in the area would also take advantage of the trappers' rendezvous by bringing goods to be traded. There was always a lot of Indian food to be eaten. The Indians taught the trappers many different games they played in their villages. The rendezvous lasted about a month and then it was time to pack up and head back to the hills, mountains, streams, and the beaver.

One of the most famous mountain men was **Jedediah Smith**, from New York. He came west as a young man and entered the fur trade. Jed was educated and carried a Bible wherever he went. He is thought to be the **first white man to go through South Pass in the Rocky Mountains**.

Jedediah Smith came to Oregon in 1828 with a party of 18 men and 300 horses. The party was moving up from California. They met some Umpqua Indians. An Indian chief stole an ox and the white men wanted it back. The ox was returned but the Indians were angry. In revenge, the Indians attacked and killed 14 trappers. The survivors made their way to Fort Vancouver, where Dr. John McLoughlin helped them. The horses were recovered along with several hundred beaver skins. Dr. John McLoughlin was indeed a big help to many mountain men and so many others who came to him for help.

FILL IN THE BLANKS:

1. The British took over _____.

2. It was renamed _____ _____.

3. The most effective lure for the beaver was

_____.

4. Out of the seven mountain men, who was the most

famous at this time_____ _____.

Joint Occupation

The War of 1812 ended with the signing of the Treaty of Ghent, in December 1814. One consequence of the war was that the Astorians sold Fort Astoria to the Nor'westers. They did so because the Nor'westers told them that they would probably have lost it anyway.

The Treaty of Ghent provided that any territory which either Great Britain or the United States acquired during the War of 1812 should be returned to its former owner. In 1815, **Secretary of State James Monroe**, saw this provision to mean that Fort Astoria, or Fort George, as it was now called, should be returned to the United States. Such a claim angered the British, for Astoria had not been taken by them in battle. The Astorians had sold it to the Nor'westers.

Two years had elapsed after James Monroe made his statement that Fort Astoria should be returned to the United States. **In 1817 an American warship, The Ontario**, sailed to Astoria under government orders and took possession of the fort and of the north shore of the Columbia River.

After taking over the fort, the United States said that the North West Company could continue to occupy and use the fort. The United States contended that the territory up to the **forty-ninth parallel** belonged to her, but she offered to let the North West Company occupy the fort until the formal agreement was signed. Great Britain accepted this arrangement temporarily, but refused to concede that the United States' claim of land went up to the forty-ninth parallel.

In the year **1818**, the **United States and Great Britain agreed to joint occupation** of the Oregon country. This agreement was to be reviewed in ten years. The area consisted of what is now **Oregon, Washington, Idaho, part of British Columbia, and parts of Wyoming and Montana.**

The winter of 1824-1825 saw growth along the Columbia River. **The Hudson's Bay Company** decided they needed a better place to locate their trading post. It was a move to anchor Britain's claim on Oregon. The site selected was on the north side of the Columbia River, near the mouth of the Willamette River. For several years mountain men, trappers, and sailors who left their ships had been settling in the Willamette Valley area close to the Columbia River. The Hudson's Bay Company felt they could establish trade with these men and win their allegiance to Britain.

DR. JOHN MC LOUGHLIN · 1784-1857
FIRST TO GOVERN THE OREGON
COUNTRY
1824-1843

The new fort was called **Fort Vancouver**. For the next 22 years, Fort Vancouver and all operations of the Hudson's Bay Company west of the Rocky Mountains were ruled by the iron will of **Dr. John McLoughlin**, called **"The Chief Factor."**

Dr. John McLoughlin was born at LaRiviere Du Loup, Canada, in 1784. John McLoughlin was a medical doctor and an energetic genius at organization. He was primarily responsible for the success of Fort Vancouver. He supervised the building of the fort, the inside buildings, his private home, the kitchen, bakery, washhouse, stockade and bastion. He saw to the building of the docks where ships could discharge their cargo of supplies and take on furs. He was the **civil government authority** over all employees in his district. Dr. McLoughlin started vegetable gardens with fields of potatoes and fields of wheat. He also planted fruit trees, all of which fed the men at the fort. There were also herds of cattle, goats, sheep and chickens.

Fort Vancouver

Fort Vancouver began to look like a small village carved out of the wilderness. Dr. John saw to it that saw mills and grain mills were built. He was always thinking of the needs of others. Because of the men taking Indian wives, Dr. John had to begin thinking of schooling for all of the children.

Yes! A school was started at Fort Vancouver. **The first teacher was John Ball. John Ball came to Oregon in 1832 with Nathaniel Wyeth**. By 1836 there were 50 pupils in the Hudson's Bay Company School.

Dr. John McLoughlin was often described as dignified and of a courtly manner. He was over six feet tall, his hair prematurely gray, was bushy, thick, and framed his face. His eyes were blue and kindly but could turn to an icy blue if

angered. He ruled the Indians with a fair but firm hand and they called him **Hyas Tyee, a good chief**. The Indians also called him **"The White-headed Eagle."**

FILL IN THE BLANKS:

1. In a._____(date) the United States and Great

   Britain agreed to joint occupancy of the

   b. _____ _____.

2. The new fort was called _____ _____.

3 Dr. John McLoughlin was called the Chief

_____.

4. Dr. John McLoughlin was over _____ feet tall.

5. The first teacher at Fort Vancouver was _____

_____.

Dr. McLoughlin conducted company affairs with dignity and treated all visitors at the fort with kindness. While it was the policy of the Hudson's Bay Company to discourage American settlements in the Oregon country, Dr. McLoughlin was always courteous to trappers, traders, and later to the missionaries and immigrants. He gave them assistance, advice and supplies. **His generosity caused him many difficulties with his superiors**.

It would seem that now Dr. McLoughlin found himself **"between a rock and a hard place."** If he continued to aid all these people he would anger his employers, yet if he did not help these people, his conscience would hurt. After many years of struggle, he made up his mind. He **resigned** from the Hudson's Bay Company in 1845 and **moved to Oregon City** on the Willamette River. There he built his home.

He moved his family into the new home in Oregon City early in 1846 and lived there until his **death in September of 1857**. Dr. McLoughlin became a **United States citizen in 1849**.

Dr. John McLoughlin could have been called the first governor of Oregon but he wasn't. On the base of his statue, located on the grounds of the State Capitol in Salem, Oregon, are written these words:

Dr. John McLoughlin
1784-1857
First to govern the Oregon Country
1824-1843.

Today we honor this great man by calling him **"The Father of Oregon."**

He was indeed a great man and friend to all men. The "Father of Oregon" title was made official in 1957 when the state legislature chose to recognize Dr. John McLoughlin's work by giving him this honorary title.

34

FILL IN THE BLANKS:

1. Explain The Treaty of Ghent _____

_____

_____

_____

_____

_____

_____

_____

.

2. In 1818 the a. _____ _____

and b. _____ _____ agreed

to joint occupation.

3. The Oregon country consisted of what is now

a._____   d. _____

b. _____   e. _____

c. _____   f. _____

4. The name of the new fort was _____

_____.

5. The chief _____was Dr.

_____ _____.

6. _____ _____ was the first school

teacher at the Fort Vancouver.

7. The Indians called Dr. McLoughlin the "White

_____ _____".

8. Was Dr. McLoughlin nice to everyone? Yes _____

No _____

9. Dr. John McLoughlin was and is called The

_____ of _____.

10. In 1845 he moved his family to a. _____

_____ and b. _____ from his

job as Chief Factor for the Hudson's Bay Company.

UNIT II

TRUE OR FALSE

1. _____ Napoleon Bonaparte was the President of the United States in 1803.

2. _____ The Louisiana Purchase was bought from France.

3. _____ President Jefferson picked Lewis and Clark to lead the expedition.

4. _____ Janey was the nickname for Sacagawea.

5. _____ Sacagawea had been kidnapped by the Blackfoot Indians.

6. _____ York was the name of Lewis's dog.

7. _____ The baby son of Sacagawea was called Pompii.

8. _____ The expedition needed canoes to cross the mountains.

9. _____ Chief Cameahwait was Janey's uncle.

10. _____ The western mountains to be crossed were called The Shining Mountains.

FILL IN THE BLANKS

11. The expedition got _____ from the Shoshone Indians.

12. The Lewis and Clark expedition was called the _____ ___ _____.

13. When all the water started flowing westward they had crossed the _____ _____.

14. Lewis and Clark built _____ _____ at the southern part of the mouth of the Columbia River.

15. The expedition spent the winter of a. _____ and b. _____ at Fort Clatsop.

16. They boiled ocean water to get _____.

17. Mountain men trapped the _____ for its fur.

18. The thick underfur was called _____.

19. Men and women wanted their _____ made from this underfur.

20. The first official trading post was built at Astoria and named after

_____ _____ _____.

21. The mountain men met once a year at

a. _____ to trade b. _____

and gather supplies.

22. Jim _____ and Jedediah Smith were two very famous mountain men.

23. Explain the "Treaty of Ghent."

_____

_____

_____

_____

_____

_____

24. r. John _____ worked for the Hudson's Bay Company.

25. Dr. John was the Chief Factor for Fort

_____.

NOW GO BACK AND STUDY ALL THE QUESTIONS FOR UNIT II TO PREPARE FOR THE FINAL TEST.

Suggested Projects

1. Using popsicle sticks or twigs, make a model of Fort Clatsop.

2. Make a teepee by using light tan material and twigs.

3. Write a report on the many animals that Lewis and Clark saw on their expedition.

4. Look in an encyclopedia and find out how a beaver pelt was cleaned and cured.

5. Visit Fort Vancouver in Vancouver, Washington.

6. Make a model of Fort Vancouver.

7. Visit Salem and see the statue of Dr. John McLoughlin.

8. Visit Astoria, Oregon.

9. Visit Fort Clatsop.

10. Visit Seaside, Oregon and find the place of the "salt camp."

Oregon History

STUDENT WORKBOOK

UNIT III

The Missionaries and the Circuit Rider Pastor—1831-1842

- *Arrival of the Missionaries*
- *End of Missionary Era*
- *Circuit Rider Pastor*

STUDENTS' GOAL	
Target Test Date	_____
Pages in Unit	_____
Pages Per Day	_____
Date Unit Completed	_____
Final Score of Unit	_____

UNIT III

The Missionaries and the Circuit Rider Pastor—1831-1842

The Missionaries Arrive

THE METHODISTS

Also I heard the voice of the Lord, saying: "Whom shall I send, and who will go for us?" Then I said, "Here am I! Send me" (Isaiah 6:8).

For years the Indian tribes of the Northwest had become accustomed to seeing the white man in their country. They saw white men who trapped the beaver. They saw the mountain men who met at Green River Valley in Wyoming at the yearly rendezvous. They watched the men of the Lewis and Clark expedition come into their area and build a place to live. The white men who worked at Fort Vancouver were all familiar sights to the Indians. They watched Dr. John McLoughlin and the white men who left their ships and settled along the Willamette River.

The Indians watched and they saw new things that greatly amazed them. They saw the white man's firearms, mirrors, the burning glass (the magnifying glass) and much more. The Indians knew of the white man's Bible.

The Indians called that book, the **Book of Heaven**. The Indians made everything they used by hand. The white man, however, had materials that were manufactured back east and brought west. All this was strange to the Indians, and they thought that the white man's religion and his Book of Heaven had something to do with his ability to produce these wonderful things. They wanted to learn about the secret of the white man's magic.

In March of 1831, four Indians (three Nez Perce and one Flathead Indian) arrived in St. Louis, Missouri. They had come to see **General William Clark**. Some Indians remembered General Clark from his journey with Meriwether Lewis in 1805. They remembered him to be an honest man and one that was fair to the Indians. General Clark was now in charge of Indian affairs in the Missouri River Valley. The Nez Perce and the Flathead Indians wanted General Clark to send white men to go back to the Indian country. They wanted white men to teach the Indians all about their Book of Heaven. They wanted some of **the white man's magic**.

General Clark reported their visit to the **Catholic Jesuits and to the Methodists**. The Methodists were holding church meetings in St. Louis at that time.

Two of the Indians died while in St. Louis. A third Indian died on his journey home and the remaining Indian was killed shortly after he reached his home village. He was killed in a raid by the Blackfoot Indian tribe.

Shortly after the Indians' visit to St. Louis, Missouri, an article appeared in the ***Christian Advocate and Journal***. Methodists read about the Indians' cry for white men to "come teach us." This article was written by William Walker, an interpreter for the Wyandotte Indians. Walker mistakenly called all four Indians, Flathead chiefs. He described how these four Flathead chiefs had walked halfway across the continent to seek the white man's Book of Heaven. He wrote how these men had been turned away unsatisfied after having come so far. Walker's article was printed along with a drawing showing how the Indians flattened their heads. This was very inaccurate, but it increased people's interest in the Indians' cause. The interesting fact was that neither the Nez Perce nor the Indians of the Flathead tribe practiced head flattening. The artist Paul Kane has left paintings, sketches and drawings show-

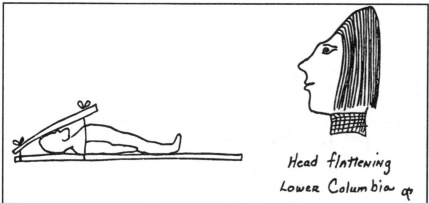

Head flattening
Lower Columbia

The interest generated by the news article and sketch of the flat-headed Indians proved fruitful. In the **spring of 1833, the Methodist Mission Board named the Reverend Jason Lee as a missionary to the Flathead Indians**. Jason Lee was a tall man, who stood 6 feet 3 inches. He was still a bachelor at the age of 30.

Lee asked his nephew, **Daniel Lee**, to accompany him on the long overland trip. He also asked **Cyrus Shepard**, who was to become **Oregon's first schoolteacher**, to go with them. They made many appearances in churches to raise the needed money to start a mission in the Oregon country. Then Lee and his party joined **Captain Nathaniel J. Wyeth**, who was leading a trading expedition bound for the Oregon country.

After a very tiring journey, Jason Lee, his nephew Daniel, and their party **arrived at Fort Vancouver on September 15, 1834**. Dr. John McLoughlin, Chief Factor of the Hudson's Bay Company, greeted them warmly.

ing that only the Cowlitz and the Chinook Indian tribes practiced head flattening. These tribes thought of it as a sign of beauty.

The head flattening process was thought to be painless and done over many months. From the birth of a baby, until the age of 8 to 12 months, he was laid on a cradleboard. The baby was strapped to the backboard, which was covered with moss or loose fibers of cedar bark. Then another short, smooth board was bound by a strap passing through holes in the backboard and up over the short board. This allowed the baby's head to be very gently molded between the two boards without pain.

FILL IN THE BLANKS:

1. The Indians of the a._____ - _____ had become accustomed to

   seeing b. _____

   _____ over the years.

2. They knew of the white man's Book of

   _____.

3. Walker's article was printed along with a drawing show-

   ing how the a. _____

   b._____ their baby's

   c._____.

4. Name the two tribes who actually did this.

   a. _____.

   b. _____.

5. Was this painful for the baby?

   Yes _____ No _____.

The Reverend Jason Lee had been sent to minister to the Flathead Indian tribes, but Dr. McLoughlin advised him that it was too dangerous. The Flatheads lived in what is today western Montana. He then advised Lee and his party to establish their mission south of the Columbia River, down the Willamette River. After much conversation, Lee agreed and moved to settle in the French Prairie area, near where the city of Salem is today. This was to be the first permanent American establishment in the Pacific Northwest.

On March 7, 1835, Cyrus Shepard opened the first school at the mission in French Prairie. The mission was trying hard to get started. Trees needed to be cut, land cleared, buildings built and crops planted. Reverend Lee saw his own need for a wife. His wife would be an example to the Indian women and would be able to help teach and care for many of the Indian children at the mission. Jason Lee wrote to the Methodist Mission Board to send more workers. He needed farmers, blacksmiths, mechanics, teachers, doctors, and carpenters. The mission board began sending the necessary people.

FILL IN THE BLANKS:

1. The Methodist Mission Board named _____

_____ _____ as a missionary to the

_____ Indians.

2. Jason Lee arrived at Fort Vancouver in the month of

_____.

3. At the advice of Dr. McLoughlin, Lee settled in

_____ _____, south of

the Columbia River.

4. The first schoolteacher for the mission was

_____ _____.

A Wife For Jason Lee

Miss Anna Maria Pittman, a 33-year-old schoolteacher from New York, accepted with great humility that she had been chosen to be the wife of the famous Jason Lee. **On July 29, 1836**, Anna traveled from Boston Harbor on the ship **Hamilton**, around the southern tip of South America at Cape Horn.

While the passengers on board were not seasick, they kept busy in many ways. They held religious services, wrote letters, and read books. They made dresses and quilts, and knitted stockings. Anna brought along a French book to help her converse with the French Canadians at the mission.

The ship proceeded into the Pacific Ocean, stopping at the **Sandwich Islands**, today called the **Hawaiian Islands**. The Hamilton arrived at the islands just two days before Christmas.

The missionaries were to stay in the Islands until a ship could be found for them that would be traveling to the Oregon country. The ship Diana was sailing eastward and took them on as passengers. **Before the ship Diana left the Islands, the Oregon-bound missionaries were asked to attend the wedding of the famous island chief, Kamehameha III to Kalama.**

Just before they sailed away from the Islands, the natives gave them presents of fresh vegetables, fruit, and some chickens.

Anna Maria **and** **Jason Lee**

Susan Downing also sailed from Boston with Anna Pittman. She was going to marry Cyrus Shepard, and help the mission. The ship Diana finally left the Islands in April and was bound for the shores of the Oregon country and the great Columbia River.

It took them another month to arrive at the mouth of the Columbia River. After finally crossing the bar at the mouth of the Columbia River, they made their way to Fort Vancouver. Word had been sent to Jason Lee in French Prairie, that a ship had been sighted just off the mouth of the Columbia River. Jason hurried to Fort Vancouver to meet his intended bride.

Anna Pittman and Susan Downing arrived at Fort Vancouver in early May. Susan Downing, Anna Pittman and Jason Lee enjoyed a week of hospitality at the fort. Dr. John McLoughlin was a wonderful host and saw to their every need. It was a good time for getting to know each other.

The time had come to head out for Mission Bottom. The first part of the trip was in a canoe, with Anna riding with Jason Lee. The second part of the journey was on horseback. They arrived at the mission only to find that Cyrus Shepard was in the middle of preparing a meal for them and was up to his elbows in the preparation.

The first meal was a wonderful one of fried venison, sausages, cheese, unbolted bread, butter, doughnuts, and tea, with strawberries and cream for dessert. They all enjoyed this sumptuous meal.

After waiting for a time to get acquainted, **Jason and Anna were married. Their wedding took place on July 16, 1837**. The Reverend Daniel Lee performed the wedding ceremony for Jason and Anna, then he stepped aside while the Reverend Jason Lee performed the marriage ceremony of Cyrus Shepard to Susan Downing. Thus, **Anna became the first white woman to marry in the Oregon country**.

After several months had passed Jason saw that the mission needed to expand. He made plans to return East to seek the needed money and support. In **March of 1838**, he left for the East.

On June 23, 1838 a baby son was born to Anna Pittman Lee. He was the first white child born in the Willamette Valley. At the Mission there was much rejoicing, but then a cloud of sadness filled the air. It was evident that the newborn son of Jason and Anna would not live long. **Two days later the baby died.** Shortly before sunrise the next day, **Anna also died.**

Thus, not only was she the first white woman to be married in Oregon, but she also became the first white woman to be buried in Oregon, with her infant son in her arms.

The sad news of the death of his wife and infant son reached Jason while he was staying at a Shawnee mission on his way east. He was grief stricken, but knew that he must continue on his journey, gathering the financial support for the mission.

Into the next year of 1839, Jason Lee worked hard. He spoke daily to Methodist churches about the Oregon mission. On a nine-week tour he raised funds for the mission amounting to almost $4,000. He made extensive trips to Philadelphia, Washington, D.C., Connecticut, and Canada.

CHRIST IS THE ONLY ANSWER

It was now time to head back to Oregon. Jason knew that he would need the support of a wife. His beloved Anna had died, but the mission would still need the example of the wife of the Reverend. Jason had met another fine lady, who felt that the Lord God was calling her to be a missionary. It was with great humility that Lucy Thomson accepted the proposal of marriage from Jason Lee. Jason took his new bride, **Lucy Thomson Lee,** back to the Oregon mission. The second Mrs. Lee made a grand and lovely contribution to the life of the mission. Lucy was ill a lot of those first few months. Less than a year after her arrival, she too died shortly after giving birth to a daughter. The daughter, named Lucy Anna Maria Lee, after Jason's two wives, lived.

The mission moved from what was called **Mission Bottom** into what is now the center of Salem. It was called **Chemeketa** at the time. A lumber and gristmill were built. Jason Lee established branch missions in places like Nisqually, on the Puget Sound; Clatsop, at the mouth of the Columbia; on the Umpqua in southern Oregon; in the Dalles; and at the falls, where Oregon City is today.

Mission Bottom

Some of the missionaries at the branch missions became disgruntled with their hard life compared with the ease of Salem living. They complained and wrote letters to the mission board back east.

In November of 1843, Jason Lee left the mission in Salem. Arriving in New York City in May of 1844, Lee hurried to the General Conference Meeting of the Methodist Church. The delegates were too busy to hear from Jason Lee.

Lee had been removed as the superintendent of the Oregon mission. The mission board was willing to reinstate him but it was too late. The new superintendent, the Reverend George Gary, had arrived in Oregon, closed the mission, and sold the property.

Jason Lee went home to Quebec and there died an unhappy man in 1845. He is now buried in Lee Memorial Cemetery in Salem. A statue of Jason Lee stands on the Oregon Capitol grounds.

On the base of the statue these words are inscribed.

Rev. Jason Lee

1803 – 1845

First Missionary

in Oregon

Colonizer

1834 - 1843

Mission Bottom does not look at all like it did in the days when Jason Lee was helping to build a permanent mission. The Willamette River has flooded many times, and the area where Mission Bottom stood is now very different.

Jason Lee did much to help shape our Oregon. It was not just an American government he wanted for Oregon **but a way of life. He wanted a commitment to be free of corruption, to have a good place to live and raise a family, and to bring the "Good News" not only to the Indians, but to all men.**

FILL IN THE BLANKS:

1. Jason Lee married a._____ _____ _____ on July b._____.

2. She was the first _____ _____ to be married in the Oregon country.

3. She was also the first white woman to _____ and be buried in the Oregon country.

4. Jason Lee's daughter was named _____ _____ _____.

5. Jason Lee wanted a way of a. _____, a commitment to be free of b. _____, to have a good place to raise a c. _____ and bring the d. _____ _____ not only to the Indians, but to all men.

The Presbyterians

But those who wait on the Lord shall renew their strength; they shall mount up with wings like eagles, they shall run and not be weary, they shall walk and not faint (Isaiah 40:31).

The Methodists were not the only good people who wanted to see the "Good News of Jesus" brought to the Indians.

Dr. Marcus Whitman was a country doctor from New York State. **Dr. Whitman** was 33 years old and wanted to help take the gospel to the Indians. Early in 1835, **Dr. Whitman**

and the Reverend Samuel Parker were sent to survey the Oregon field. The American Board of Foreign Missions sent the men. The American Board represented Congregationalist, Presbyterian, and Dutch Reformed churches.

The men made the trip by going with a fur trading expedition. Their expedition was headed for the annual rendezvous at Green River. The good doctor helped with the trail work. He put his shoulder to the mired-down wagons, and helped build bridges and rafts. All of this won him the grudging respect of the tough mountain men.

It was the quick actions of Dr. Whitman that lives were saved when cholera struck the men of the camp. For twelve days and nights he battled the disease. He lost only three men, and the rest were very grateful to the doctor for saving their lives.

The expedition finally arrived at the rendezvous on the Green River. Here they met **Jim Bridger and Kit Carson**. These two men were famous mountain men. During the time spent on the Green River, Dr. Whitman had time to talk to the Indians who were at the rendezvous. He saw that they were eager to learn from the white man. He saw some wild celebrations at the rendezvous that convinced him of the Indians' need for help.

Before he left, Dr. Whitman gained the admiration of one very famous mountain man. Jim Bridger had been struck by an iron-barbed arrowhead three years earlier. It had lodged in his back, and he had carried it there all those years. He had found no one he trusted to take out the arrowhead. **Dr. Whitman operated**, with the trappers and Indians watching his every move. **He removed a three-inch arrowhead from Jim Bridger's back**. After this, his medical talents were in much demand.

The Reverend Parker decided to go west to look over possible sites for a mission. Meanwhile Dr. Whitman headed back east to recruit workers and gather materials.

On February 18, 1836, Dr. Marcus Whitman married Narcissa Prentiss. Narcissa was 27 years old, well educated, and felt called of God to be a missionary to the Indians. The long journey across the country was to be a honeymoon for Narcissa and Marcus.

At Cincinnati, Ohio, the Whitmans met their trail companions, the stern **Reverend Henry H. Spalding and his sad-eyed wife, Eliza**. Eliza and Narcissa faced a hard journey of almost 2,000 miles. They took a steamboat for the journey to St. Louis, Missouri, and from there they went up the Missouri River to Liberty, Missouri. Here they switched to a heavy wagon. They were trying to reach the American Fur Company's caravan. Thomas Fitzpatrick led the caravan. The Whitmans and the Spaldings finally caught up with Fitzpatrick and the caravan. The hard trip west had begun. Narcissa Whitman kept a diary. In this diary we can read about her trip west. **From 6 A.M. until 6 P.M.** they traveled, sometimes in the wagons, sometimes on horseback, and sometimes walking. They called that **"going on shanks mare."**

Narcissa and Marcus Whitman

Narcissa's diary stated, "Start usually at 6, travel till eleven, encamp, rest and feed, start again about two, travel until six or before, then encamp for the night." Narcissa noted in her diary how thrilled the ladies were when they arrived at Fort Laramie. It was the first time they were able to do a good-size load of laundry. She noted the hardship of trying to take such a large wagon across the country. She also said that the ladies also rode horseback from time to time.

FILL IN THE BLANKS:

1. The name of the 33-year-old doctor was _____

_____.

2. Dr. Whitman saved lives when what disease hit the

camp? _____

3. A three-inch barbed a. _____

was removed from the back of b. _____

_____.

4. Dr. Whitman married _____

_____.

The missionaries stopped just long enough to scratch their names on **Independence Rock**. In time this was called the **register** of the Oregon Trail. Then they were on the trail and headed west once again.

On the **fourth of July,1836**, the missionaries came to the **top of South Pass**. They had crossed the **Continental Divide**. Stories have been told that they got down off their horses and knelt. They held a **Bible in one hand** and the **American flag** in the other. They **thanked God** for a safe journey thus far.

Although this event was not recorded, this was how it was remembered many years later.

The party spent some time at the Green River rendezvous. Narcissa was very popular with all of the Indian women because of her blonde hair. Dr. Whitman was to meet the Reverend Samuel Parker at the Rendezvous, but Parker was not there. Parker was still exploring the upper Columbia River and sent word that the Whitman party should continue west with the men of the Hudson's Bay Company.

Marcus had hoped to take his wagon all the way to the Columbia River but was unable to do so because of rough ground. They reached **Fort Hall** and by now the **wagon** had become a two-wheeled cart, due to a splintered axletree. Beyond Fort Hall they lost the trail, got caught in swampland, and were attacked by swarms of mosquitoes. Two weeks later they reached **Fort Boise**. It was here that Dr. Whitman finally abandoned the cart. Another three hard weeks of travel brought them to **Fort Walla Walla**. After a swift boat trip down the Columbia River, they finally arrived safely at Fort Vancouver. Dr. John McLoughlin welcomed them warmly to the area. As Dr. McLoughlin was making the newcomers welcome and comfortable, he told them that the Reverend Samuel Parker had sailed for the east coast.

Dr. John McLoughlin spent much time with Dr. Whitman and the Reverend Spalding. He helped supply them with much needed provisions. The Spaldings would settle among the Nez Perce Indian tribes in what is now Idaho.

Against the advice of Dr. McLoughlin, Dr. Whitman and Narcissa would build their mission among the Cayuse Indian tribes at a place called Waiilatpu or "Place of the Rye Grass."

FILL IN THE BLANKS:

1. Names were scratched on a. _____

   _____, and in time it was called the

   b. "_____" of the Oregon Trail.

2. At South Pass they had crossed the

   _____ _____.

3. At Fort _____ Dr. Whitman finally abandoned the cart.

4. The Spaldings settled among what Indian tribe?

   _____.

5. The Whitmans settled among what Indian tribe?

   _____.

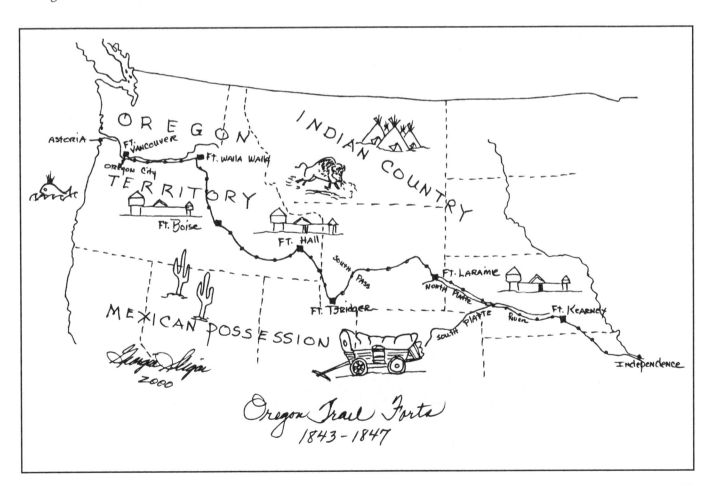

Oregon Trail Forts
1843 - 1847

43

Whitman Mission at Waiilatpu

sions were made. They would teach the Indians in their native language as well as English. They accepted a **printing press from the Hawaiian Mission in the Hawaiian Islands**. This would help them to begin printing in the native language of the Nez Perce. The printing press was kept at Lapwai. In all, eight books in the Nez Perce language were printed.

Narcissa and Eliza were the first white women to cross the Continental Divide. The wagon did not make it. It would be 1840 before Marcus Whitman would see a wagon that had gone over the mountains pull into the mission yard at Waiilatpu.

Now the heavy daily work began. The land had to be cleared, and a home had to be built. They had to have a barn for the cattle, a sawmill, a gristmill, and many other outbuildings. In addition, a well needed to be dug if they were to have a supply of water. They did not look forward to carrying water from a stream or river.

A baby girl was born to Narcissa and Marcus on March 14, 1837. She was the first white child born in the Northwest. (Remember that the baby boy born to Jason Lee and Anna Marie Pittman Lee was born on June 23, 1838). The Indians called Alice Clarissa the **white fawn**.

A school at the mission had been started that first winter of 1836. The spring of 1837 found Dr. Whitman and Narcissa conducting classes. They themselves were trying to learn the Indian language. They also spent time ministering to the sick of both the Indians and the whites at Lapwai and Waiilatpu. They held church services and ministered to the needs of all who came to them.

Reinforcements arrived in August 1838. Another missionary party arrived to assist the Spaldings and the Whitmans. Those who came were the Reverend and Mrs. Cushing Eels, the Reverend and Mrs. A.B. Smith and an unmarried young man by the name of Cornelius Rogers.

A meeting was held and several important deci-

Among the books printed were an **eight-page primer**, and an **eight-page booklet containing the laws of the Nez Perce** that were adopted by the Nez Perce at Lapwai in December of 1842. Also printed was a **32-page hymn book**. In 1845, the Reverend Spalding printed his translation of the Gospel of Matthew.

*March 14, 1837- Alice Clarissa Whitman was the first white child born in the Northwest.

*June 23, 1838- Jason and Anna Lee's baby boy was the first white child born in the Willamette Valley.

FILL IN THE BLANKS:

1. Narcissa and Eliza were the first white women to cross the _____ _____.

2. The Whitmans had a daughter and named her _____ _____.

3. The Indians called her _____ _____.

4. A printing press was sent from the_____ Islands mission.

5. Books in the _____ _____ language were printed.

Catholic Missionaries

Two years after Jason Lee set up his mission in the Willamette Valley, the **French Canadians** living in the area asked Dr. John McLoughlin to send for a **Catholic priest**. They wanted the priest to instruct them in their own religion. Dr. McLoughlin forwarded their petition to the bishop of the Catholic church in the city of Quebec.

The Hudson's Bay Company expressed strong doubts about the wisdom of allowing priests to come into the Willamette settlement. They felt that the activities of Protestants and Catholics might lead to trouble with the Indians. They felt it might be too confusing to the Indians.

Dr. McLoughlin thought the priests might prevent the Americans from having an influence over the Canadians. Reluctantly, the Hudson's Bay Company gave permission for the priests to go to the Oregon country, on the condition that they would not start a mission south of the Columbia River. They must do all of their ministering to the French Canadian trappers and mountain men, north of the Columbia River. The priests felt they should be able to minister anywhere they wanted, not limited to one area.

The first Catholic priest to arrive in November 1838 was Father Francis Norbert Blanchet. His assistant was Father Modesti Demers. The two priests' work was primarily among the French Canadians. But soon they began to minister to more and more of the local Indians.

The priests founded Mission St. Francis Xavier in the Cowlitz Valley. Father Demers also went on mission trips to Walla Walla, Colville, and the Okanogan. **Father Blanchet stayed at French Prairie**, near present-day Salem. It was the largest parish south of the Columbia River. In January 1839 he dedicated St. Paul's Mission. In **1842 St. Joseph's school for boys was founded. In 1844 the Sisters of the Congregation of Notre Dame de Namur started a school for girls.**

In 1843, the Catholic church promoted **Father Blanchet to a bishop**. He was then made an archbishop. His headquarters were in Oregon City.

The work among the Indians was left to the Jesuit fathers. **Father Peter John DeSmet, a 39-year-old Belgian, was to minister to the Flathead Indians at the headwaters of the Missouri River**. He was encouraged to see the Indians' desire to learn. The Catholic priests worked mainly with the unspoiled tribes of the Interior.

By 1850, the Catholic community in the Willamette Valley had dwindled. Many French Canadians had sold their land to the Americans and moved away. Many followed the gold rush into California, southern Oregon, and Montana.

The missionary era of the Pacific Northwest from 1834 to 1843 was not only one of spiritual activities. It was also a period of building a colony in which religious faith was important.

FILL IN THE BLANKS:

1. The first a. _____ priest to arrive was

   Father b. _____.

2. Father Blanchet stayed at _____

   _____.

3. The priests ministered mainly to _____

   _____.

4. Father DeSmet was going to minister to the

   _____ Indians at the headwaters

   of the Missouri River.

Life at the Whitman mission was hard. **Little Alice Clarissa Whitman drowned** in the Walla Walla River when she was two years old. The Whitmans were grief stricken, but continued to minister to the Indians.

In 1842, the Board of Missions in Boston became dissatisfied over the expense of maintaining the missions of the Oregon country. They were going to make some changes. At this time it was decided that Marcus would journey back to Boston and appeal to the Mission Board. It was September, almost too late to make it across the snow-covered mountains, but he made it. When he arrived in Boston, Marcus was able to convince the Mission Board to continue its support of the existing Oregon country missions.

He also talked to government officials about Oregon. In **Washington, D.C.**, he talked to **Secretary of State Daniel Webster**. He urged congressmen to establish **more forts along the trail to Oregon**. These forts would help protect the people traveling west. More and more people were making the trip to the Oregon country. In **New York City he saw Horace Greeley** and got Greeley's support for the Oregon cause. Greeley was a journalist for the New York Tribune. Some historians say that **Marcus Whitman "saved" Oregon for the United States**. He drew attention to the fact that if the United States would not settle the Oregon region, then the British would move in and take it over for themselves.

At this time we must go back to Oregon. We leave Marcus Whitman in New York with Horace Greeley. We shall return to him shortly.

FILL IN THE BLANKS:

1. How old was Alice Clarissa Whitman when she

   drowned? _____

2. In Washington, D.C., Marcus talked to Secretary of

   State a. _____ _____. In

   New York City, he saw b. _____

   _____.

3. Whitman urged congressmen to establish more

   _____ along the trail.

4. Some historians say that Marcus Whitman

   "_____" the Oregon country from

   the British.

Using your dictionary, define the following:

5. **missionary** _____

   _____

   _____

   _____.

6. **commitment** _____

   _____

   _____

   _____.

7. **cholera** _____

   _____

   _____

   _____

   _____.

8. **manufacture** _____

   _____

   _____

   _____.

9. **accompany** _____

   _____

   _____

   _____.

10. **establish** _____

    _____

    _____

    _____.

11. **disgruntled** _____

    _____

    _____

    _____.

12. **respect** _____

    _____

    _____

    _____.

13. **register** _____

    _____

    _____

    _____.

14. **encourage** _____

    _____

    _____

    _____

Dr. Marcus Whitman returned to the mission at Waiilatpu. He continued to minister to the Cayuse Indians. The doctor and his wife spent their time trying to teach the Indians to read the Word of God. The Whitmans tried to teach the Indians the morals and manners of the white man, but the Indians only wanted the "magic" of the white man's Book of Heaven. They did not want the discipline or hard work.

Tomahas

Eventually the Cayuse Indians began to wonder what the Whitmans were doing for them. The mission crops were feeding the white settlers. The wagon trains kept coming into the Cayuse land and they were fed at the mission. The Indians were upset that all these white people were trampling on the Indian land and the Indian pride.

The white man had brought this sickness called measles. Smallpox, dysentery and influenza were other diseases that affected the Indians, adults and children alike.

Finally in **November 1847**, the Cayuse Indians became incensed at the Whitmans' success in healing the white children suffering from smallpox, and failing to heal the Indian children. The Indians had no resistance to measles or other diseases.

The Cayuse were now going to make Marcus and Narcissa pay the price of the Indian shaman who fails to cure. That price was death.

One of the Indian children who had died belonged to **Chief Tiloukaikt**, who had already lost two other children to the "white man's sickness." The chief was outraged and plotted the death of the Whitmans.

The Whitmans were having a quiet evening at home on November 29, 1847. Chief Tiloukaikt entered the Whitman home. While he engaged Dr. Whitman in conversation, **a warrior, Tomahas,** struck the doctor from behind. By the time the killing was over, there were 13 dead, including the daughter of Joe Meek. Several orphaned children from a wagon train, who were staying with the Whitmans, escaped (the Sager Sisters). The Whitman massacre brought the missionary era to a close. The Spaldings and other Presbyterian missionaries fled for their lives. The influence of the Catholic priests also was affected. Many people blamed the priests for being too easy on the Indians. The priests had ignored the thievery and lying of the Indians. The Catholic effort with the Indians never was the same again.

And how shall they preach unless they are sent? As it is written: "How beautiful are the feet of those who preach the gospel of peace, Who bring glad tidings of good things!" (Romans 10:15).

The Circuit Rider Pastor

From the time that God moved on men to bring the "**Good News of the Gospel**" to others, there have been those who went above and beyond the call of duty. These men were known as the "**Visiting Pastor**" or the "**Circuit Rider Pastor**." These brave men came across the mountains with their families. They settled in an area, cleared their land, built their houses, planted their crops, and traveled many miles. The miles they traveled led them to families who wanted to hear the Jesus of the Bible preached, even though they did not live anywhere close to a church or a mission.

Many people came across the Oregon Trail during the great migration of 1843. These people did not always settle in groups. Many of the families traveling to the Oregon country came because they would receive free land. Each man would stake his claim on a piece of land and then begin to settle down. They were spread out from the Blue Mountains all the way to the Applegate Trail in southern Oregon.

Many families have the diaries of their family histories. The stories detail what the family endured to travel the Oregon Trail. Their hardships often included the pain of the death of a loved one, or the leaving of some of their furniture and belongings along the trail. The diaries contain the details of how the Circuit Rider Pastor would make his rounds to visit families.

The pastor would leave his family, and head out on the trail. His first stop might be to a neighbor who lived just 20 miles away. He might stay in the barn with the livestock, or he might be put up in the loft bedroom with the children of the family. They would have their singing time, the reading of the Bible, then the pastor might pray for the sick. If the weather permitted, he might baptize any new converts to Christ. What was his pay? Well, he could be paid with a dozen eggs, or a live chicken, or maybe an armful of corn. The poor pastor would not be able to carry all of this with him as he continued on his route. Sometimes as he made his return trip home he would stop off at these farms and collect whatever the people wanted to give him. The **pastor would never ask for money**. He would just be blessed by sharing the Word of God.

The pastor would ford streams, dodge wild animals, and fight the cold wind and rain, ice and snow. He had to make a camp, start a fire to cook a meager dinner, sleep on the cold ground, and try to escape the fear of getting lost in the wilderness. All of this was done with joy in the knowledge that he was bringing the Bible and the Word of God to people who might not otherwise hear the gospel.

BALD EAGLE

The Circuit Rider Pastor was instrumental in starting many churches and sowing the seed of the gospel. He followed the "**Golden Rule**." He had high ideals and admonished the people to **fear God and to keep His commandments**.

Many of the old names in Oregon have had the Circuit Rider Pastor as an ancestor. Some of the names would be **Powell, Clark, Atkinson, Raymond, Brewer, Bryan, Holmes, Fletcher, Harvey, Bayliss, Whiteside, Nesmith, Booth,** and so many, many more.

Many of these families boasted of family members being **pastors, doctors, teachers, pharmacists, university instructors, engineers, lumberjacks, high school principals, bankers,** and more. All contributed to the growth and development of the Oregon country, making it a better place to live.

To read more about the first families of Oregon, go to your local **historical society**. There are many books written about these first families. **Maybe there are one or two Circuit Rider Pastors in your family**.

FILL IN THE BLANKS:

1. The Whitmans tried to teach the Indians

   a._____and

   b. _____.

2. The Indians did not want the

   a. _____ b. _____.

3. Name the four diseases the white man brought into the Indian country.

   a._____ c. _____

   b._____ d. _____

4. On November a. _____ the b. _____ Indians became incensed at the Whitmans.

5. The Indians had _____ _____ to these diseases.

6. Name the Indian who struck Dr. Whitman from behind

   _____.

7. How many people were killed at the mission? _____

8. What is another name for the Visiting Pastor?

   "_____ _____ _____."

9. Did the pastor ever ask for money?

   Yes _____ no _____.

10. The Circuit Rider Pastor followed the_____

    _____.

11. He had high a. _____ and admonished the

    people to b._____ _____and to

    c._____ his _____.

12. All of these pastors contributed to the growth of the Oregon country to make it a better

    _____ to _____.

MATCHING

a. Mission Bottom   f. Narcissa Prentiss

b. Jason Lee   g. Anna Maria Pittman

c. Book of Heaven   h. Waiilatpu

d. Marcus Whitman   i. Cowlitz & Chinook

e. Doctor   j. Independence Rock

1. _____ The Indians wanted to find the white man's Bible called?

2. _____ The first white preacher to become a missionary to the Flathead Indians.

3. _____ The two tribes that really flattened the heads of babies.

4. _____ Jason Lee married?

5. _____ Lee built his mission at?

6. _____ A Presbyterian minister?

7. _____ Whitman was a?

8. _____ Whitman married?

9. _____ The rock everyone on the wagon train signed was called?

10. _____ The Whitmans settled at what place?

FILL IN THE BLANKS

11. The Methodist missionary was? _____ _____.

12. The Presbyterian missionary was? ____ _____ _____.

13. The first Catholic missionary was? _____ _____ _____.

14. Dr. and Mrs. Whitman settled in a place called Waiilatpu which means "_____ ___ _____ _____ _____."

15. The Whitmans were missionaries to the _____ Indian tribe.

16. Where did Father Blanchet settle? _____ _____.

17. A printing press was sent to the mission from where? _____ _____.

18. Dr. Whitman saw _____ _____ in New York City.

19. Dr. Whitman urged congressmen to build more _____ along the Oregon Trail.

20. Who was the Cayuse warrior who struck Dr. Whitman from behind? _____.

21. At the Whitman massacre there were _____ killed.

22. Was Joe Meek's daughter killed? _____yes ____ no.

23. The name of _____ _____ _____ was given to the preacher who went from home to home to teach the "Good News."

24. This pastor always tried to follow the "_____ _____."

25. He had high ideals and admonished the people to "fear God and to _____ _____ _____."

NOW GO BACK AND STUDY ALL THE QUESTIONS FOR UNIT III TO PREPARE FOR THE FINAL TEST.

Suggested Projects

1. In your Bible concordance, find as many scriptures as you can about spreading the Word of God. Check out the places where Jesus went and the places where Paul went.

2. Find a map showing the North and South American continents and draw a map showing the route that Anna Maria Pittman traveled to Oregon.

3. What were some of the things that an old country doctor might have in his bag?

4. Make a model of Fort Hall, Fort Boise, Fort Walla Walla or Fort Vancouver, using popsicle sticks or twigs.

5. Find a picture of Independence Rock. Make a model using clay or flour and water. While it is still soft, sign names in the surface of it. Sign your name.

6. Visit the Whitman Mission National Historic Site in Walla Walla, Washington.

7. Visit your local historical society and get more information on any missionaries that preached in your area.

Oregon History

S T U D E N T   W O R K B O O K

UNIT IV

The Oregon Trail, Wagon Trains & Wolf Meetings—1843-1858

- *Beginnings of a Provisional Government*
- *The Great Emigration*
- *Gold*

STUDENTS' GOAL	
Target Test Date	_____
Pages in Unit	_____
Pages Per Day	_____
Date Unit Completed	_____
Final Score of Unit	_____

UNIT IV
The Oregon Trail, Wagon Trains & Wolf Meetings—1843-1858

Let every soul be subject to the governing authorities. For there is no authority except from God, and the authorities that exist are appointed by God. (Romans 13:1-3).

Write out verses two and three:

Vs. 2 _____

_____

_____

_____

_____

_____

Vs. 3 _____

_____

_____

_____

_____

The Beginnings of a Provisional Government

IN THE OREGON COUNTRY

We need to step back a few years. In **1838**, and again in **1840**, a handful of settlers living in the Willamette Valley petitioned the United States Congress to extend the protection of the laws and courts from back east to the Oregon country. Congress took no action.

Then in **1841, the death of one man changed the** course of history in our area. That man was **Ewing Young**. Ewing Young was a mountain man and a fur trapper who had come to Oregon in 1834. He settled in the Chehalem Valley. He brought a lot of cattle in from California. **Ewing Young built the first sawmill in the Willamette Valley**. The mill was located on Chehalem Creek. He became a very rich man.

When Ewing Young died, he was a wealthy landowner who had no family or heirs to inherit his wealth. The men of the area, his friends, got together to decide what to do with Young's estate. Laws were needed but there were none in the Oregon country. How was his property to be divided? Who was to get what? Who would take all the cattle, the land and the sawmill?

Meetings were held to persuade the United States government to declare the Oregon country as a **provisional government**. The settlers wanted more than to settle the estate of one man.

The **Reverend Jason Lee** was chosen, along with other men of the area, to discuss ways of bringing law to the Oregon country. These men were selected to draft laws for the settlement south of the Columbia River. **Dr. Ira Babcock** was instructed **to act as supreme judge** with probate powers to administer the estate of Ewing Young. Dr. Babcock was to act according to the **laws of New York State**, until regular laws could be adopted for Oregon.

At this time the British at Fort Vancouver and the Hudson's Bay Company did not want any laws of the United States interfering with their business in the Northwest. They wanted to keep things the way they were, with both the United States and the British sharing the area.

The settlers wanted to keep the real reason for their meetings secret from the British. They wanted to establish some form of United States government. **The British were told that the settlers were meeting to discuss the wolves that had been**

killing the livestock in the area. The British knew that the wolves had indeed been a problem. So they did not try to stop the meetings. Thus the meetings became known as the "**Wolf Meetings**."

JOE MEEK

On May 2, 1843, Marcus Whitman was getting ready to return to Oregon from New York. Back home in Oregon, a man by the name of **Joe Meek** was shouting during an important meeting. Joe Meek was a mountain man, fur trapper, and a tall storyteller. Joe talked to the men at the meeting held at **Champoeg, Oregon country**. They had been having meetings for a long time. Enough was enough! Some of the men wanted the British to rule and some of the men wanted the United States to rule the Oregon country. Now they must vote. Finally Joe shouted, "**Who's for a divide? All in favor of the report and organization, follow me**." Joe was asking how many men were in favor of the United States to govern the Oregon country by making it a provisional government. It was hoped that this temporary government would lead to Oregon becoming a territory of the United States.

As Joe shouted, "**Who's for a divide**?" The men parted. Some men sided with Joe and others hung back. When all noses were counted the vote was 52 to 50. It was a close vote but just enough. The Americans had won with two votes to spare. We now had the first American government established on the Pacific Coast. The meeting was held at Champoeg.

The new government was little more than a name, but it was strengthened by the selection of a judge, a sheriff, and a treasurer at a **July 1843** meeting. **Joe Meek was elected to be the new sheriff. George Abernethy was voted in as governor**.

Now **five counties** were formed. They were named **Clackamas, Champoeg, Yamhill, Tualatin, and Clatsop**. They called their laws "**The First Organic Laws**." Oregon City was made the first capital of the provisional government. The area began to grow, and people began to pour into the Oregon country.

FILL IN THE BLANKS:

1. The death of _____ _____ in 1841 was to change the course of history in our area.

2. At a meeting _____ _____ was chosen along with other men of the area to discuss ways of bringing _____ to the Oregon country.

3. These meetings became known as the "_____ _____."

4. Joe Meek was elected _____.

5. The first capital was located at _____ _____.

Using your dictionary, define the following:

6. **optimism** _____

_____

_____

7. **curiosity** _____

_____

_____

_____

8. **parallel** _____

_____

_____

_____

9. **inherit** _____

_____

_____

_____

10. **ransom** _____

_____

_____

_____

11. **epidemic** _____

_____

_____

12. **emigrants** _____

_____

_____

_____

The Great Emigration of 1843

Doctor Marcus Whitman was now making ready for his return trip to Oregon. At Elm Grove, a short distance from Independence, Missouri, a large wagon train was forming for the trip west.

On May 22, 1843, the wagons left Elm Grove, Missouri. There were more than 120 wagons, 200 families consisting of 1000 people, and 3000 head of cattle. This was the first of a long procession of wagon trains that was to wind its way across the prairies and over the mountains. The deep

wagon ruts they would cut into the land heading west would be called The Oregon Trail. **This became the first highway to the Northwest.**

Land was a big reason that families came to Oregon. Most were driven to seek new lands not because of greed or self-gain but for three good reasons. **First, a pioneering instinct; second, optimism that life is good and will get better; third, curiosity that life was good but what great things might lie over the next hill?** (Americans today are still the most traveled people on earth.)

The people prepared for the trip. These were the first people to make the crossing with such a large party of wagons, families and cattle. Others would learn much from them. They would learn what to take and what to leave behind.

They needed to buy many things for the trip, and had to learn exactly how much of each item should be purchased.

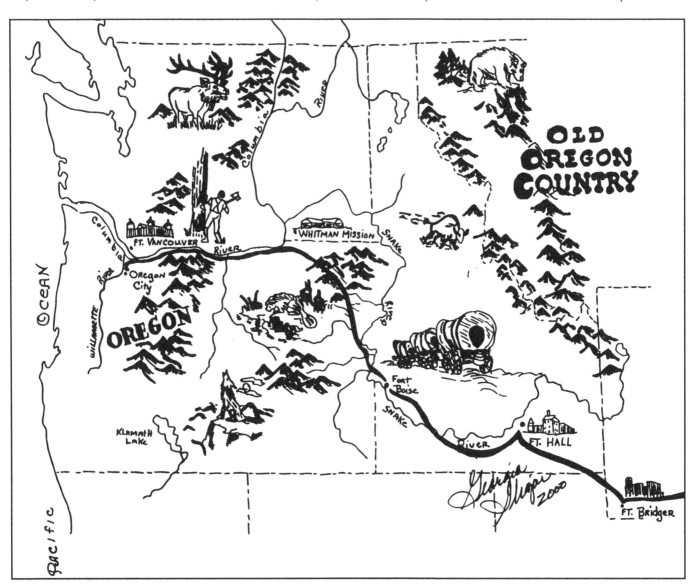

They bought sturdy wagons and a team of oxen. They needed the oxen instead of horses. Ox teams withstood the trip better because they were much less trouble than horses and were less likely to be stolen by the Indians. Men would take horses, but not for the pulling of these large wagons.

To the right is a list of food to be taken for a family of five people to last for five or more months. The cost was about $150 not including the cost of the wagon and the oxen.

Also needed were cooking utensils of cast metal, plates and cups of tinware, two churns, one for sweet milk and one for sour milk, tools to build a house or repair a wagon, an awl, shovel, augers, saws, crosscut saw, and a good supply of rope.

Each person was to be supplied with every kind of clothing, for warm weather and also for cool to cold weather. They would need heavy boots and shoes. Each male should have at least one good rifle and one shotgun with a good supply of ammunition.

The wagon train passed many places along the trail that are now famous: **Chimney Rock, Scotts Bluff, Fort Laramie, Independence Rock** (where they paused to carve their names in the soft rock), **South Pass, Fort Boise, Grande Ronde, The**

Columbia River, The Dalles, Barlow Road, Fort Vancouver, and Oregon City, to name a few.

FOOD LIST

800 lbs. flour	5 lbs. pepper
100 lbs. ham	5 bushels dried apples
100 lbs. bacon	50 lbs. rice
60 lbs. dried beef	3 gallons vinegar
26 lbs. cheese	2 lbs. pilot bread
20 lbs. tallow	1 bushel beans
1 lb. ginger	3 gallons pickles
13 lbs. tea	6 lbs. mustard
2 sacks salt	10-gallon keg of water
3 lbs. allspice	5 lbs. saleraties (sodium bicarbonate, baking soda or aerated salt)
5 lbs. tartaric acid	
100 lbs. sugar	

At one time along the trail millions of buffalo blanketed the Great Plains. By the late 1860s their numbers had already been drastically reduced. They had died off with the competition from horses for winter fodder, from diseases carried by the emigrants' oxen, and loss of grasslands to the overland trails. They were hunted for their meat by the fur trappers and then to feed the crews of the railroad. They also were killed by the Indians themselves for their hides to make warm buffalo robes. **The Indians used almost every part of the buffalo. They made clothes, moccasins, parts of their teepees, and a lot more. It has been said that the buffalo was the life of the Indian.**

Fill in the blanks:

1. On _____ 22, _____ the wagons left Elm Grove, Missouri.

2. Name the three reasons families came to Oregon.

   a. _____

   b _____

   c. _____

3. _____ were used to pull the wagons.

4. The cost for a family of five was $ _____, not including the oxen and wagon.

5. Each male should have a _____ and a

   _____.

6. Name some places they passed along the trail.

   _____

   _____

   _____

   _____

All in all, it took **five months or more** to make the trip. They traveled **nearly 2,000 miles**. Many arrived just as winter was beginning to put her white coat on Mount Hood. If they arrived late they would have to battle the snow on Mount Hood or brave the raging rapids of the Columbia River. Many suffered on the long journey. Battered, bruised, exhausted, hungry, wet, cold, and sometimes disheartened, they nevertheless continued on till they reached their goal. Their goal was the Oregon country that was to be their new home.

When the wagon trains arrived at The Dalles they saw a raging Columbia River. Today, with the system of dams built along the great Columbia River, we no longer see the swift raging water with the rapids that existed back in 1843. The dams that have been built have made the river very tame. One place that has been lost used to be a place where the Indians fished, called **Celilo Falls**. These falls were where the Indians fished for the great **Chinook salmon**. The Indians used the meat from the salmon as the main food in their diet. Today, Bonneville Dam has "fish ladders" that help the salmon reach the upper parts of the Columbia River.

Dr. Marcus Whitman accompanied this wagon train of 1843. He helped everywhere he was needed, from repairing wagon wheels to bringing new babies into the world. He was there to help the emigrants keep safe from the four greatest hazards of the trail.

1. grizzly bears

2. rattlesnakes

3. cholera

4. getting lost

FILL IN THE BLANKS:

1. It took _____ or more months to make the trip.

2. The four greatest hazards of the trail were:

   a. _____

   b. _____

   c. _____

   d. _____

55

Use a red pen or crayon and mark the trail from Independence to Oregon City.
Use a green pen or crayon to mark all the forts along the trail.

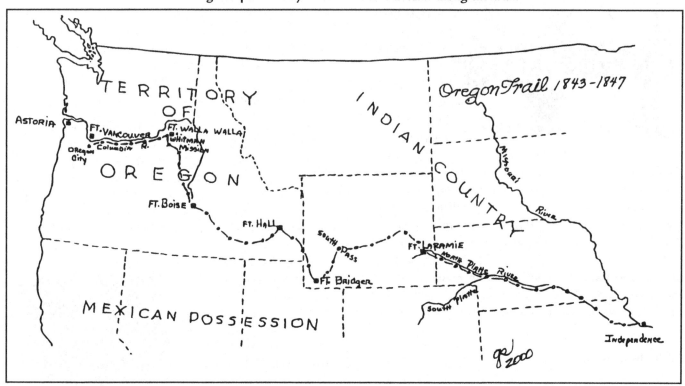

Oregon Trail 1843 – 1847

On The Trail

This wagon train was so large that they had to separate the train into smaller units. The number of cattle was so great that the cattle had to travel on a trail parallel to the wagons but several miles away, mostly because of all the dust kicked up by the cattle and wagons.

Special men were selected to ride with the cattle to herd them and keep them from stampeding. **Jesse Applegate** was one of the many men who rode with the cattle. You can read his famous account of his travels, entitled "*A Day with the Cow Column,*" at your local library.

Jesse Applegate also wrote that Dr. Whitman's great experience and indomitable energy were of priceless value to the wagon train.

The wagon train averaged about 12 to 15 miles a day. They crossed many rivers, but when they crossed the **Platte River** they said it was so muddy that it flowed "**bottom side up.**" The Platte was also known as being **"a mile wide and an inch deep, too thick to drink and too thin to cut."**

When they reached **Fort Laramie** they rested. The wagon train had covered 667 miles in 40 days. They pushed on across the dry plains in the broiling hot sun. Bear Meadows was also a good resting place. Many families were facing starvation by the time they reached Fort Hall. Supplies were gathered and then they all pushed onward. It took 40 men with axes four days to get over the Blue Mountains. Almost there! Almost there! This was the cry heard throughout the wagon train. The Dalles! Now they still had to get around Mount Hood.

As the settlers rode rafts down the churning Columbia River, they knew they had almost reached their goal. When they arrived in the "**city by the falls,**" Oregon City, they were welcomed. They had arrived not to a wild place but to a place where a provisional government had been set up with a judge and a sheriff. They could now begin to build their homes and farm the land.

Dr. Whitman had brought the "Great Emigration of 1843" into Oregon. He could now go back to his wife and his ministry at **Waiilatpu**.

FILL IN THE BLANKS:

1. a. _____ _____ wrote the now

   famous account entitled   b . "A Day _____

   _____ _____ _____."

2. The wagon train traveled about _____ to _____

   miles a day.

3. The a. _____ _____ was so muddy

   it was said to flow b. _____ _____

   _____.

4. The settlers rode a. _____ down the churning

   b._____ _____.

5. Dr. Whitman brought the "_____

   _____" of 1843 into Oregon.

Interesting Story of 1844

There are so many stories of families coming across our country on wagon trains. Many of our "First Families of Oregon" have had their stories told and re-told or written in books. These books allow all of us to know what it was really like to be on a wagon, fording rivers, crossing mountains, dodging buffalo herds, and tending to the sick.

Here I will share one such story about a famous family, the Sagers. Henry Sager, his wife, and six children were preparing to join a wagon train in early 1844. They were in St. Joseph, Missouri, and joined a group of eager pioneers who called themselves the **"Independent Colony." There were 323 people and 72 wagons in the party**.

They continued on the trail heading into eastern Kansas only to find the prairies had turned to mud and the rivers so swollen that it was too dangerous to cross. There were problems with the oxen and an unrealistic fear of Indians.

About five weeks out of St. Joseph, Missouri, Mrs. Sager gave birth to her seventh child. Mrs. Sager was in a weakened condition and soon caught a cold that she was unable to shake. Going on, they came to the fording place of the South Platte River. Mr. Sager lost control of his oxen, the wagon overturned, and Mrs. Sager was injured.

One of the daughters, young Catherine, broke her leg as she tried to jump off of the wagon. Her dress caught on the wagon and the large wheel of the wagon rolled over her leg. It was badly broken, but a doctor with the group put a splint on it and she proceeded on the trip.

Weeks passed. A sickness called "camp fever" struck the members of the wagon train. Mr. Sager and three of the children came down with the fever. In a very short time **Mr. Sager died** and was hastily buried alongside the trail.

Somewhere along the Snake River, Mrs. Sager became much worse with the "fever." She died shortly after the wagon train stopped for the evening. Mrs. Sager was buried, wrapped in a sheet, along the trail. **Mr. And Mrs. Sager died within twenty-six days of each other.** The children were now without a father or a mother. What was to become of them?

The men and women of the wagon train took it upon themselves to look after the seven orphaned Sager children.

It was now nearing the end of September and the wagon train encountered the first snow in the mountains. Soon they arrived at a place in the trail near the Whitman mission. One of the men rode on ahead and got to the mission in time to ask the Whitmans to take in the Sager children.

Narcissa and Marcus had lost their own sweet daughter, and they already had taken in several of the Indian children, as well as the children of some of the mountain men. They felt they could take care of all but the two youngest, but at the last minute, they took all seven. The Whitmans felt that the Lord had given them a mission to take care of any and all children who came across their path.

The Sager children stayed with Narcissa and Marcus, from the fall of 1844 till the tragic killing of the Whitmans on November 29, 1847. Among those killed were two of the Sager boys, along with the daughters of Joe Meek and Jim

Bridger. Another Sager daughter was ill with measles at the time of the massacre, and died soon afterwards from lack of medical attention.

The four Sager children who survived were Catherine, Elizabeth, Matilda, and Henrietta. They all grew to adulthood. Catherine became a schoolteacher, Elizabeth taught school prior to getting married and having eight children. Matilda went into ranching with her husband. Henrietta entered the theater as an actress.

To read more stories about families who came over on the Oregon Trail or over the Applegate Trail, go to your local library and check in the Oregon history section. You can also visit your local historical society.

Therefore submit yourselves to every ordinance of man for the Lord's sake, whether to the king as supreme to governors, as to those who are sent by him for the punishment of evildoers and for the praise of those who do good (I Peter 2: 13 & 14).

54° 40´ Or Fight

Where should the line be drawn to divide the land the British would rule and the land the American government would rule?

In **early May of 1844, James K. Polk was nominated for President of the United States.** He wanted the United States to be bigger. Why not buy or take California from Mexico? Why not claim Oregon all the way up to 54 degrees – 40 minutes on the line with the Russian Territory? So the cry went out, **"54° 40' or fight" (54 degrees 40 minutes north latitude.)** James K. Polk was

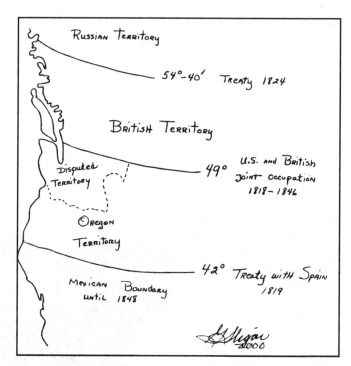

LATITUDE:

LONGITUDE:

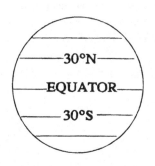

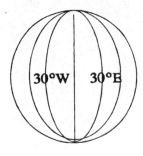

elected in November of 1844 and took office in January of 1845.

The population of Oregon was growing with each year's wagon train arrival. As more and more people moved to Oregon they wanted a good government and more land. **Approximately 1,000 people came into the Oregon coun-**

try in 1843, another 1,400 people in 1844, and 5,000 more by 1845. Pressure was again put on Congress to annex the Pacific Northwest.

Tension was also growing between the British and American settlers and there were some wild threats to burn Fort Vancouver.

In the summer of 1845, British and American warships were sent to the Pacific Coast. The question on many lips was, "Would there be war?" Who could forget the famous cry of Joe Meek, "54° 40' or fight"?

President Polk now made recommendations to Congress that the United States give Britain notice of her intention to terminate the treaty of joint occupation at the end of one year. He also recommended that **a chain of forts be constructed to protect the wagon trains moving west.**

FILL IN THE BLANKS:

1. a. _____ __ _____ was elected President in

   b. _____ of 1844 and took office in January of c.

   _____.

2. _____ people came to Oregon in 1843.

3. _____ people came in 1844.

4. _____ people came in 1845.

5. President Polk recommended that a chain of

   a. _____ be constructed to protect the

   b. _____ _____ moving west.

6. Using your Bible, write out the verses from

   Isaiah 49: 11 & 12 _____

   _____

   _____

   _____

   _____

   _____

   _____

   _____

   _____.

Barlow Road

Samuel K. Barlow, age 55, came to the Oregon country with the 1845 wagon train. Most of the emigrants didn't arrive at The Dalles until late in September. They found many people waiting for a raft or boat to take them to Oregon City. They also would have to pay for the trip and many were not going to be able to afford the expense. The trip was dangerous, taking them over rapids and rough water. Many families had lost wagons, oxen, horses, cows, and all of their goods in the rapids.

Using a red pen or crayon, trace the Barlow Road from Boyd to Oregon City.

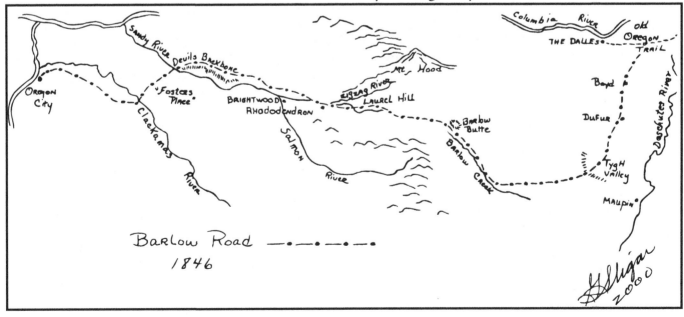

Barlow Road —•—•—•—
1846

Mount Hood stood in the way. There was no road around the southern slopes of the mountain. This would have to change.

Sam Barlow said, "God never made a mountain but what He provided a place for man to go over or around it". So he would go over or around Mount Hood.

Sam Barlow and William Rector, with several wagons, their families and their livestock pulled out of The Dalles in early October. The party headed south through the **Tygh Valley**, the ancestral home of the Tygh Indians.

Joel Palmer, leading another party of wagons, was trying to catch up with Sam Barlow. **Barlow and Palmer met and decided to continue around the mountain to the southwest**. The going was very rough. It was a path that only the Indians used, covered with large rocks, trees fallen across the trail, and a lot of brush. Horses could get around all of this easily, but wagons needed the path cleared.

Winter was threatening and each man knew that they soon must make a decision. Should the wagons be left? Should they push on and be caught by heavy snows? They decided to leave the wagons and go on to Oregon City on foot and horseback. Their supplies were running low, and now they must hurry. There was no time to spend trying to clear a path for the wagons.

Sam Barlow and William Rector left the party and headed for Oregon City to get food to bring back to the others. Securing the needed provisions, Barlow and Rector returned, to the joy and relief of the party.

All saw that it would be impossible to get the wagons out that winter. The west slopes of the mountain were very heavy with trees, very deep canyons, steep rocky hills and many swift streams.

By now William Rector's wife was ill and he was worried about her safety. He decided to return to The Dalles. It is likely that a few other families joined the Rectors' trip back to The Dalles.

Meanwhile Sam Barlow and the others found a place to leave the wagons. They called the place "Fort Deposit."

William Berry volunteered to spend the winter guarding the wagons.

Fill in the answers to the following:

1. Sam Barlow said "God

   _____

   _____

   _____

   _____."

2. The party headed south through the _____

   _____.

3. William _____ took his ill wife back to The

   Dalles.

4. The wagons were left at a place called " _____

   _____."

5. _____ _____ volunteered

   to stay with the wagons.

The party began the last leg of their journey to Oregon City. Barlow went on ahead of the party to try to get some food to bring back. He found Phillip Foster's house, rested a short while, was given food and was on his way back to rejoin the party when he found them very near the Foster cabin.

The Sam Barlow, Joel Palmer party arrived in Oregon City on Christmas Day, 1845. It had been a very long, tiring journey.

Barlow petitioned the provisional government for a charter to construct a wagon road across the Cascade Range, around Mount Hood to Oregon City. He thought it would cost about **$4,000**. Building the road would cost a lot more. Barlow started construction on the road in the spring of 1846. Phillip Foster was to be his partner.

The Barlow Road was a very difficult road to build. There were miles of thickets to cut through, swamps to smooth over, hillsides to grade, streams to cross and re-cross, and heavy stands of fir, cedar, and pine to penetrate.

The new road was to be a **toll road**. The toll was set at **$5.00 for each wagon, 10 cents for each loose oxen, horse, or mule. In the 1860s the toll was lowered to $2.50 per wagon.**

The first wagons to travel over the new road were those left at Fort Deposit. Their owners brought them out in July 1846. **The first emigrant to come over the Barlow Road was J.W. Ladd, who arrived in the provisional capital of Oregon City on September 13, 1846.**

In the spring of 1846, as Barlow was building his road, the British were formally notified of the termination of the joint occupation of the Oregon country.

Sam Barlow finished what he set out to do. He had built a road around a mountain. Barlow died in 1867, and his final resting place is a small cemetery in the town of Barlow.

FILL IN THE BLANKS:

1. a._____ _____ constructed the road in the

   spring of b._____.

2. _____ _____ was his partner.

3. The toll for a wagon was $ _____.

4. Later it was lowered to $ _____.

5. The first emigrant to come over the Barlow Road was

   ____ _____ _____.

The thought of 54° 40' was still there, but when the British representative, Lord Aberdeen, proposed that the boundary be located at the **49th (degree) parallel** Congress accepted. **On August 5, 1846, the agreement became official and ended a 28-year-period of joint occupancy of the Oregon country.**

It took the settlers of Oregon about six months to receive the news. No war! Great joy and celebration took place. The people thought that the government would make the Oregon country into a territorial region right away. As a territory the people would have United States laws, backed by the authority of a federal government. It would also mean that there would be the protection of Army troops against Indian attacks. The people would also have a representative in Congress to help them with local concerns.

The **Provisional Governor, George Abernethy,** appointed **J. Quinn Thornton to be the territorial delegate to Congress.** Thornton's job was to try to get some action in getting Oregon territorial status.

The year was 1847, and the biggest concern in Congress at the moment was the question of slavery. The settlers of Oregon had made it clear in the "**First Organic Laws,**" that they wanted no part with slavery. Furthermore, they wanted no blacks in Oregon, either as slaves or as free men. The southern states opposed any state that did not want slavery. Their opposition resulted in the defeat of a bill introduced to Congress to make Oregon a territory.

FILL IN THE BLANKS:

1. The British representative, Lord a._____

   proposed the boundary to be located at b._____

   parallel.

2. The Provisional Governor a. _____

   _____appointed b._____ _____

   _____as a delegate to

   Congress.

3. The settlers made it clear that they wanted no part with

   _____.

Back In Oregon

Since the white man's arrival in the Oregon country, they had, unknowingly, been bringing sickness with them. The Indians had no natural immunity against **the diseases of small pox, cholera, measles, and many others were brought to the Oregon country.** In just a few short years these diseases had wiped out a large portion of

A dramatic drawing shows a grim Indian assaulting Marcus Whitman while his wife tries to stop him. Actually, Narcissa rushed in after her husband had already been wounded.

each tribe and village. It is estimated that at the time of Dr. John McLoughlin's arrival in 1824, there were **100,000 Indians**. By the late 1840s their numbers had been reduced to around **30,000**. For this the Indians blamed the white man and, as is nearly always the case, they hurt those trying to help them.

For 11 years Dr. Whitman had helped the Cayuse Indians but without much success. When the epidemic of measles hit, the Indians were dying but the whites were not affected. Three of **Chief Tiloukaikt's** own children died from the disease.

The Indians' resentment smoldered against the whites. It all exploded on **November 29, 1847**.

After Dr. Whitman held a funeral, Chief Tiloukaikt, along with others, entered the mission kitchen at Waiilatpu. While **Chief Tiloukaikt** engaged Whitman in conversation, a warrior, **Tomahas**, struck Whitman from behind. When the slaughter was over, **13 whites** staying at the mission lay dead, among them Dr. and Mrs. Whitman.

There are many speculations as to what caused the Indians

to attack the Whitmans. Some thought that the Cayuse blamed the doctor for leading the 1843 wagon train into their country. Others felt the missionaries were trying to urge the Indians **to give up their nomadic ways and settle down to raise crops, go to school, and attend church.** The missionaries also tried to get the Indians to **give up the practice of having more than one wife.** Another theory posed was that the difference between the doctrine of the Protestants and the doctrine of the Catholics confused the Indians, adding to their dislike of the white man.

Probably the biggest reason for the hostility of the Indians was the **epidemic of measles**. The measles killed hundreds of Indians in the summer and fall of 1847. The Indians believed that a medicine man could bring death as well as life to anyone. **Dr. Whitman was a white medicine man**.

Two Cayuse Indians, Chief Tiloukaikt and Tomahas, were the main leaders. **Dr. and Narcissa Whitman were killed on November 29, 1847**, along with 11 others. **Joe Meek**, the mountain man, now sheriff, had his little **daughter, Helen**, at the mission at Waiilatpu. Little Helen was killed along with the others.

FILL IN THE BLANKS:

1. Diseases the white man brought were

   a. _____ b._____

   c. _____ .

2. In 1824 there were an estimated _____ Indians.

3. In the 1840s their numbers had declined to

   _____ .

4. The _____ Indians attacked and killed Dr. and

   Mrs. _____ along with _____ others.

5. Joe Meek's daughter, _____, was also killed.

6. The Indians thought of Dr. Whitman as a white

   _____ _____ .

The Indians held captive 45 women and children. One ten-year-old girl held captive was Eliza Spalding, the daughter of the Reverend and Mrs. Henry Spalding.

Messengers were sent to Fort Vancouver and help was soon on the way. **Peter Skene Ogden of the Hudson's Bay Company** went to Fort Walla Walla and called a meeting of all the Indian chiefs in the region. **He told them he would pay a ransom for the captives. By January 1848, all of the captives had been freed and Eliza Spalding was reunited with her parents.**

The provisional government needed help from the United States Congress. An Indian rebellion was threatening the Oregon settlement. The legislature decided to **send Joe Meek to Washington, D.C.** He was to carry the story of the massacre and plead for aid.

Joe Meek was the man to send. He was not only a teller of tall tales but a great talker. He was said to have talked the bark off a tree. If the Indians had named him they probably would have called him "Chief Flap Jaw of the Loose Mouth Tribe." Yes, Joe was a talker. **He was also a cousin to President James Polk.** He would be the one to go to Washington, D.C.

Arriving in Washington in the spring of 1848, Joe talked to everyone about Oregon, the Indians, the massacre, and the need for immediate action.

Finally on August 14, 1848, President Polk signed the bill creating Oregon as a U.S. territory. The boundaries were to the 49th parallel to the north, and the 42nd parallel to the south, the continental divide to the east, and the Pacific Ocean to the west.

President Polk appointed **General Joseph Lane as Oregon's first territorial governor**. To the office of **territorial marshal**, the president appointed **Joe Meek.**

Governor Lane and Joe Meek headed home to Oregon, arriving just one day before President Polk retired from office.

For six years, from 1843-1849, **Oregon City** was the capital of the **provisional government**. Then it was the **capital of the territorial government for one year, from 1849 to 1850.**

FILL IN THE BLANKS:

1. Ten-year-old _____ _____ was held captive by the Indians.

2. The legislature sent _____ _____to Washington, D.C.

3. Joe was a cousin to _____ _____.

4. What were the four boundaries for the Oregon territory?

   a. _____

   b. _____

   c. _____

   d. _____

5. Who was the first territorial governor ?

   _____   _____.

6. Joe Meek was appointed as the territorial

   _____.

The Cayuse Indians who were guilty of the Whitman massacre, along with Chief Tiloukaikt and Tomahas, surrendered, and were tried and hanged by Marshall Joe Meek in 1850.

The **population** of the Oregon Territory was growing. Each year brought arrivals on the wagon trains.

1843 — 1,000	**1845 — 5,000**	**1847 — 4,500**
1844 — 1,400	**1846 — 1,350**	**1850 – 12,093**

The first federal census taken in Oregon Territory revealed that in 1850 there was a population of over 13,000 people.

(When the year 2000 census comes out, check the population numbers for your city, county, and the state as a whole.)

Samuel Thurston was Oregon's first territorial delegate to Washington, D.C. He helped persuade Congress to pass the **Donation Land Act of 1850. This law gave 320 acres of land to each adult male. If married, his wife also received 320 acres.** This much land was given to settlers who arrived in Oregon before 1850. Those who arrived in Oregon after 1850 were given only 160 acres, or 320 acres per married couple. The Donation Land Act expired in 1858, but many families moved into the Oregon Territory to homestead before the deadline.

In the decade of the 1850s there were many skirmishes between the Indians and the new settlers who wanted to take away their land. The white man made treaties with the Indians, then promptly broke the treaties.

Gold had been discovered in 1849 in California and touched off a rush of men going through Indian tribal lands. **There were incidents of the Rogues, Klamaths, and Modoc Indians** defending their lands and families from these white men seeking gold.

FILL IN THE BLANKS:

1. The first federal census in Oregon Territory revealed that in 1850 there were over _____ people.

2. The Donation Land Act of 1850 gave an adult male a._____ acres and his wife got b._____ acres of land.

3. The Indians defended their a. _____and families from white men seeking b. _____.

4. _____was discovered in California in 1849.

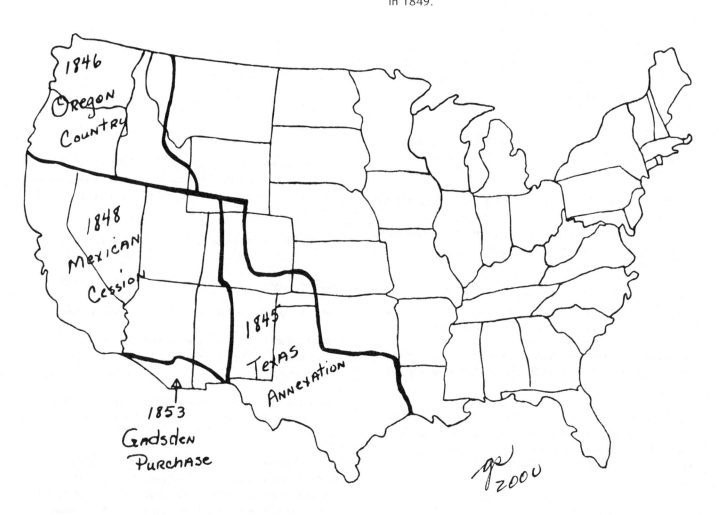

64

WRITE A LETTER.

You have just come over the Oregon Trail and have settled in Oregon. Write a letter telling about your trip to a grandparent, an aunt, a cousin or maybe a best friend back on the East Coast.

September 29, 1843

Dear _____

_____

_____

_____

_____

_____

_____

_____

_____

_____

_____

_____

_____

_____

_____

_____

_____

_____

_____

_____

_____

_____

_____

Very truly yours,

_____

PSALMS 119:127

Write this Scripture on these lines.

_____

_____

_____

_____.

Gold, Gold, Gold

Gold was discovered in southern Oregon in 1852 in the town of Jacksonville. The discovery of gold in any area would draw men like a magnet—men seeking to get rich in a hurry.

The fear of the Lord is clean, enduring forever; the judgments of the Lord are true and righteous altogether. More to be desired are they than gold, yes, than much fine gold; sweeter also than honey and the honeycomb (Psalms 19: 9 & 10).

The word spread quickly. Gold was found lying in the streams, waiting to be picked up. In no time at all, several thousand men were in and around Jacksonville staking claims.

The miners were a tough bunch who survived on the barest amount of supplies. All supplies had to be brought in by wagon or pack mule. Sometimes it was a long time before more supplies arrived. **The winter of 1853** was a harsh one on the miners. **They had to endure hunger, Indian attacks, fires, floods, small pox epidemics, and a shortage of salt.**

The miners worked hard and sweated a lot. They needed to replace the salt their bodies lost. **There was a time in Jacksonville that salt was more sought after than gold. Many a man would pay a pouch of gold for a pouch of salt.**

"You are the salt of the earth" (**Matthew 5:13**). *(From your Bible, fill in the rest of this Scripture).*

_____

_____

_____

_____

_____

_____

_____

_____.

Many stories have come out of the gold mining days. Here are a few:

There is the story of the schoolchildren. Yes, there was a school in Jacksonville. A lot of the miners brought their wives and children with them. The children attended school.

As the town of Jacksonville grew, a railroad was built between Medford and Jacksonville to bring in supplies. The town of Jacksonville was higher in elevation than Medford, so the train engine had to work up more steam to pull itself up the steep grade.

Now the schoolchildren come into the picture. Sometimes the older boys would become bored and looked for things to do. They discovered that if they greased the railroad tracks at a certain point, the wheels of the locomotive would begin spinning. Then, as they watched, the train would begin to slide very slowly backwards. The engineer would open the engine all the way, but the train would continue to slide back toward Medford. This was in 1891.

FILL IN THE BLANKS:

1. Gold was discovered in the town of _____

in southern Oregon.

2. Miners were a a._____ bunch of men who survived on the barest of b._____.

3. The winter of _____ was a harsh one.

4. There was a time that a._____ was more sought

   after than b._____.

5. The Jacksonville schoolchildren _____ the rail-

   road tracks.

The prisoners in the town jail missed several meals because their jailer was out working his claim. The prisoners decided to dig their way out of jail. In the process they struck gold. When the jailer came back to let them out, the men didn't want to go. The jailer couldn't figure out why they didn't want to leave.

Another time when the Oregon tax collector arrived in Jacksonville, the miners said they lived in California. The California/Oregon border was nearby and

created confusion. When the California tax collector arrived, all the men said they lived in Oregon.

Between 1853 and 1880 more than $13 million in gold dust passed through the little bank in Jacksonville, operated by C.C. Beekman.

During this era 5,438 mining locations were registered in Jackson County. There were 16 copper mines, one tin mine, 124 cinnabar mines, and all the rest were for gold and silver mines.

To understand a little about gold mining, we'll take a look at just a couple of methods. Mining falls into two categories: **"placer" or "hardrock." Placer was the most common method, using water.**

There is one simple fact. Gold is heavier than the earth substances that surround it.

Placer

Panning was the most primitive method of placer mining. A miner would simply take a large pan, put in gold-bearing earth, add water, slosh the mixture around until the gold settled to the bottom, then he let the other material spill over the edge of the pan.

The **rocker** method was developed to increase production. The rocker looks a lot like a baby cradle. Dirt is shoveled in and water added as the rocker is moved from side to side. The water, dirt and other materials pass over the sides while the gold settles to the bottom.

THE CRADLE OR ROCKER

The sluice box was better than the rocker or panning. The sluice box is a long trough with small cleats fixed at intervals along its bottom. A continuous stream of water is run into one end of the box. Then gold-bearing dirt is shoveled in. The water washes away the dirt that is worthless. The gold sinks to the bottom of the box and is caught by the cleats.

FILL IN THE BLANKS:

1. Between 1853 and 1880 more than

   $_____ in gold dust passed

   through the bank in Jacksonville.

2. Name several types of mines:

   a. _____ d. _____

   b. _____ e._____

   c. _____

3. What was the most primitive type of mining?

   _____

4. The _____ looks like a baby cradle.

Hardrock

The **second type** of gold mining in and around Jacksonville was called **hardrock**. This method had to be used where the gold was not loose, but encased in quartz. The quartz was dynamited or broken up with a pick. The rock was then hauled to a stomp mill, where giant hammers would smash the larger rocks into smaller bits. Once the rock was crushed, the ore was processed, either as in placer mining, or by use of chemicals to retrieve the gold.

After several years the rich veins began to run out. Then large **dredges** and **hydraulic mining** came into use. Great streams of high-pressure water shot through hoses directed at hillsides. The earth and gold were washed down to sluices where the gold was extracted.

The dredges were used a lot in the Baker and Bourne areas of eastern Oregon. These dredges would move along a

stream bed sucking up large quantities of gold-bearing material. The gold was extracted and the waste was dumped to the side of the stream. The waste was called "tailings." Piles of these tailings can be seen today along many streams in southwestern Oregon, near Jacksonville, and in eastern Oregon near Bourne.

Between 1862 and 1872 in Grant County, south of John Day, $8 million worth of gold was mined.

Three types of gold found in Oregon were:
1. gold dust   2. gold flakes   3. gold nuggets

Look in your local newspaper to find the current price for one troy ounce of gold in today's market.

Back in the 1850s, gold was worth about $35. a troy ounce.		
1850s — $35.00	1970s — $34.85	1984 — $377.50
1950s — $35.00	1980 — $850.00	1985 — $304.20
1960s — $35.00	1982 — $371.50	1999 — $293.20

Check your local daily newspaper for the current price of one troy ounce of gold in today's market.

Blue Bucket Mine

There is a story that goes like this. A wagon train heading for The Dalles and Oregon City took a short cut. They thought it was a quicker way around the Blue Mountains, and not so rough. It was the Meek Cutoff, named after Stephen Meek (the brother of our Joe Meek, mountain man/sheriff/marshal).

The short cut was very hard and the party of pioneers almost died. Somewhere along the way they finally found good water. They stopped for several days beside this stream, resting. While the adults rested, the children played. Early one morning a small boy was beside the stream playing with his small blue bucket. His mother called for him to hurry as the wagon train was leaving. "Hurry, child, hurry," said his mother. A couple of shiny rocks caught his attention. As he bent to pick them up, his mother called again, and he turned and ran to the wagon, clutching his shiny rocks. He jumped into the back of the wagon as it headed for The Dalles.

This was in 1845 and gold was not discovered until 1852. Years later the shiny rocks were brought out and identified as gold, but no one could remember where they had camped when the small boy picked up the shiny rocks. All the boy could remember was that he had left his small blue bucket by a stream.

For years men have looked for a place where a blue bucket would show them gold nuggets as large as small oranges. Somewhere out there is the Blue Bucket Mine.

FILL IN THE BLANKS:

1. Great streams of high-pressure _____ were directed at hillsides.

2. _____ were used a lot in the Baker and Bourne areas.

3. The waste was called _____.

4. Name three types of gold found in Oregon.

   a._____ b. _____

   c. _____

5. For years men have looked for the lost _____

   _____ _____.

6. The nuggets they would find would be as large as small

   _____.

The Chinese

The Chinese were important, especially to the miners. Chinese immigrants worked very hard in and around the gold towns. They would often work for as little as **25 cents a day**. Their day started at 4 AM and continued until about 10 PM.

The Chinese themselves never really tried to fit in. They came from a different country, their clothing was different, their language was different, their skin color was different, and they wore their hair in one long pigtail that hung down their back. Yes, they were different, but very hard workers.

WRITE OUT ISAIAH 45:12:

_____

_____

_____

_____

_____

_____

_____ .

Most of them had left their families back in China and were sending most of their wages home.

They kept to themselves. Nearly every mining town had its own Chinatown. The Chinese men built churches or temples for themselves, called **"Joss houses."** They tried to stay out of trouble and socialized among themselves.

FILL IN THE BLANKS:

1. The _____ were important.

2. They often worked for as little as _____ a day.

3. Every mining town had its own_____.

4. The Chinese men built churches or temples for themselves called

   "_____ _____."

MULTIPLE CHOICE
(CIRCLE THE CORRECT ANSWER)

1. The death of one man changed the course of history for Oregon.
   a. Joe Meek   b. Ewing Young   c. Jim Bridger

2. The secret meetings were called?
   a. Secret society
   b. Fort member meet-ings
   c. Wolf meetings

3. Joe Meek was elected to what office?
   a. president
   b. mayor   c. sheriff

4. The first capital was located at?
   a. Oregon City
   b. Salem
   c. Newburg

5. What animal was used most to pull the wagons?
   a. mules   b. horses   c. oxen

6. There were three reasons families came to Oregon: pio-neering instinct, optimism, and
   a. greed   b. foolishness   c. curiosity

7. Most wagon trains left Elm Grove or Independence, Missouri around,
   a. February   b. May   c. September

8. The basic cost for one family, not count-ing the cost of wagon and oxen was?
   a. $5,000   b. $500
   c. $150

9. Jesse Applegate wrote
   a. The River Crossing   b. A Day with the Cow Column
   c. How the West was Won.

10. What famous river was called so muddy that it flowed bottom side up?
    a. Missouri
    b. Columbia   c. Platte

FILL IN THE BLANKS

11. James K. _____ was the president in 1845.

12. The president wanted more _____ to be built along the wagon train trail.

13. _____ _____ was going to build a road around Mount Hood.

14. Small pox,
    a. _____ and
    b. _____ were some of the diseases brought to Oregon by the white man.

15. Who was the first territorial governor? _____ _____.

16. Joe Meek was the sheriff but now he was appointed the territorial _____.

17. The Donation Land Grant gave _____ acres of land to every adult male.

18. The Indians were defending their land from white men seeking to get rich by finding _____.

19. When mining for gold, there were two methods:
    a. _____   b. _____.

20. Name the three types of gold.
    a. _____   b. _____
    c. _____.

21. For years men have looked for the lost " _____ _____ _____."

70

NOW GO BACK AND STUDY ALL THE QUESTIONS FOR UNIT IV TO PREPARE FOR THE FINAL TEST.

Suggested Projects

1. Make a relief map using flour and water. Put in all the forts along the Oregon Trail.

2. Make a fort using popsicle sticks or twigs. Pick a fort from along the trail.

3. Using an empty milk carton, make a wagon using the picture as your guide.

4. Using resource material from your local library, do a 250-word report on any of the following:

   A Day with the Cow Column

   Dams built along the Columbia River

   Chinook Salmon and their lives

   Building a road around a Mountain

5. Check your local library or the Internet for the population for your city, county and state. Compare these numbers with the census figures of the Oregon territory in 1850.

Oregon History

STUDENT WORKBOOK

UNIT V

Government and Statehood—1859

· *Steamboats*
· *Indian Wars*
· *Women's Suffrage*

STUDENTS' GOAL	
Target Test Date	_____
Pages in Unit	_____
Pages Per Day	_____
Date Unit Completed	_____
Final Score of Unit	_____

UNIT V

Government and Statehood 1859

For we are God's fellow workers; you are God's field, you are God's building. According to the grace of God which was given to me, as a wise master builder I have laid the foundation, and another builds on it. But let each one take heed how he builds on it. For no other foundation can anyone lay than that which is laid, which is Jesus Christ. Now if anyone builds on this foundation with gold, silver, precious stones, wood, hay, straw, each one's work will become manifest; for the Day will declare it, because it will be revealed by fire; and the fire will test each one's work, of what sort it is. If anyone's work which he has built on it endures, he will receive a reward. If anyone's work is burned, he will suffer loss; but he himself will be saved, yet so as through fire (I Corinthians 3:9-15).

A New State

The year is **1859**, the date is **Valentine's Day, February 14. President James Buchanan** has just signed a bill making **Oregon the 33rd state** of the Union. **John Whiteaker was elected the first governor** of the state. The city of **Salem** was chosen to be the new capital of Oregon.

During this time Portland, located on the west bank of the Willamette River, was a growing town. Portland went through a period of time when it was called "**Stumptown,**" because of all the tree stumps left standing. The stumps had not been dug out and were left in the ground. Since the wagons rode high over the large wagon wheels, there was no need, just yet, to dig the stumps out. Hence, the nickname Stumptown.

In **1845** Stumptown was to get a new name. Two men, **Francis Pettygrove of Portland, Maine, and Asa Lovejoy of Boston, Massachusetts flipped a coin. Pettygrove won the toss.** Stumptown was renamed Portland, Oregon. By the toss of a coin, we could have had the name of Boston, Oregon.

The Steamboats

About the same time that gold was being discovered in eastern Oregon, 1861, men saw the need for better travel. For many years the only way of travel to the Oregon country and Portland, was by horse, canoe, ships on the Columbia River, flatboats, rafts, wagons, and "shanks mare."

"Shanks mare" was walking on one's own legs. A gentleman by the name of **John C. Ainsworth** was a riverboat captain on the Mississippi River. Captain Ainsworth came to Oregon and took over the steamboat, *Lot Whitcomb*. The *Lot Whitcomb* was the first steamboat built on the Willamette River.

Captain Ainsworth started his own company in 1860. He called it the **Oregon Steam Navigation Company**. Very often a steamboat could earn from $3,000 to $5,000 profit on a single trip. **A record was set in 1862 by a single steamboat earning $10,000 for just one trip**. Many carried 10,500 passengers in one year and then three years later they carried 36,000 passengers. **Steamboats were coming of age**. Travel was getting better than the canoes of the Indians or the pirogues that Lewis and Clark used as they traveled west along the Columbia River. Steamboats were the best way to travel if you lived near a waterway.

FILL IN THE BLANKS:

1. On February 14, a. _____, President

   b. _____ signed a bill

   making Oregon the c. _____ state

   of the United States.

2. _____ was made the new capital.

3. The old nickname for Portland was

   _____.

4. Mr. Pettygrove and Mr. _____ flipped a coin

   to rename "Stumptown."

5. The _____ _____ was the first

   steamboat to be built on the Willamette River.

6. Captain a._____ started his own

   company in 1860. He named it the

   b. _____

   _____.

7. A record was set in 1862 by a single steamboat

   earning $ _____ dollars for just one trip.

Indian Wars

The Indians' battles with the white man go back many years. Books have been written about these battles. Here we will study only three battles. **The first is the Rogue River War, the second is the Modoc War and the third is the Nez Perce War**.

To study these and other Indian wars in depth, go to your local library for books on these subjects.

The battles may date back to when the white man first stepped on Indian land in Jamestown, Virginia, in 1606. Let us take a look at just what happened in Oregon.

ROGUE RIVER WAR

When gold was discovered in and around Jacksonville, in southern Oregon, the Rogue River Indians became hostile. The Indians attacked the settlers and miners. They looted and burned the miners' cabins and killed or drove off the settlers' livestock. **The worst battle took place in 1856 at Gold Beach**, where 25 to 30 settlers were massacred. A detachment of United States Army troops from California came into southern Oregon to rescue the trapped settlers. The Rogue River Indians were then made to move onto an Indian reservation. This same Indian reservation was also the home for the Grande Ronde and Siletz Indians. The reservations were areas of land set aside for the purpose of giving the Indian tribes special places to live.

MODOC WAR

In **1864**, the **Modoc and Klamath Indians** were moved onto the Klamath Indian Reservation near the Klamath Lake area.

The Klamath Indians lived along the Klamath River and the Modoc Indians lived just east of there. In the years long past they had all belonged to the same tribe. Now they lived apart and frequently warred with each other. Neither the Klamaths nor the Modocs were happy about sharing the same reservation.

One of the Modoc subchiefs was Captain Jack. Captain Jack decided to leave the Klamath Reservation area and head back to their old land on the border between Oregon and California, in the Tulelake region near Lassen Peak. About 200 men, women, and children went with him. Later they were all persuaded to return to the reservation by Captain Jack's sister, Mary. **Mary was often called "Queen of the Modocs" by the settlers**.

The Indians tried to get along with each other but were soon quarreling over campsites and ownership of timber.

In **1870, Captain Jack** and nearly the entire tribe left the reservation to go back to their old lands along Lost Creek. For two years, the superintendent of Indian Affairs tried to get the Modocs to return, but without success. Finally in the fall of 1872, orders were received from Washington, D.C. to make the Indians go back to the reservation or else. Soldiers were sent to carry out the order.

Captain Jack

Captain Jack requested a conference to talk to the soldiers. During the conference, Captain Jack and many others laid aside their weapons. All except one, **Scarface Charlie**, refused to lay down his weapons. As the soldiers tried to take a gun away from Scarface Charlie, he fired the gun and the battle was on.

The battle dragged on for weeks, then months. The Indians set up camp in the lava beds south of the Oregon and California border. The lava beds are very rough volcanic areas that are criss-crossed with natural trenches and caves. Some of these trenches and caves are quite deep. The Modocs could hide easily. The Indians would leave the lava beds to attack a nearby settlement, then escape back into the almost impassable terrain.

Captain Jack and about 60 warriors held off a party of over 500 soldiers. The battle stretched into five months. Captain Jack really wanted peace. He grew tired of all the fighting and urged his people to put an end to it. Hope was in the air.

Another peace conference was called. General Edward Canby, Alfred Meacham, the Reverend Eleazer Thomas, LeRoy Dyer, the Indian agent from Klamath, and others attended. Frank Riddle and his wife Tobey were the interpreters. At the meeting with Captain Jack were other tribal chiefs. Some of these tribal chiefs were Boston Charley, Shacknasty Jim, Bogus Charley, Black Jim, Ellen's Man, Schonchin John and Hooker Jim.

A tent was set up between the army lines and the Indian stronghold. Everyone was in place to discuss peace. No one knew what his motives were, but all of a sudden Captain Jack drew his gun and shot General Canby through the head. Boston Charley shot the Reverend Thomas. Schonchin John then fired a shot at Alfred Meacham. Meacham was wounded and the others escaped to the army lines.

After this unprovoked attack, the army sent in reinforcements to go after the Modoc Indians. The Indians were greatly outnumbered, but this time the lava beds did not give them the needed protection. The Modocs began to argue among themselves. They finally split into two groups. The two groups of Indians left the lava beds with the soldiers close behind.

On June 1, 1873, the soldiers captured Captain Jack, and the other Modocs surrendered. Following a military trial in October, Captain Jack, Schonchin Jim, Black Jim and Boston Charley were hanged. Other leaders were sentenced to life imprisonment. Many of those imprisoned for life were sent to the prison in Oklahoma.

FILL IN THE BLANKS:

1. Name the three Indian wars we studied :

   _____

   _____

   _____

2. What Indian tribe around Jacksonville became

   hostile? _____.

3. The worst battle of the Rogue Indians was in what year?

   a._____ at what place?

   b._____

4. The most famous Modoc Indian was

   _____.

5. Captain Jack's sister was named

   _____.

6. She was often called _____

   _____ _____ _____.

7. The general that Captain Jack shot was

   _____ _____.

NEZ PERCE WAR

The old name of *Shahaptain* was no longer used. The name given to the Indians who wore ornaments pierced in their nostrils became **Nez Perce**. They were so named by the **French Canadian trappers**.

The Nez Perce tribe was divided into smaller bands, with each band having its own chief. Old Chief Joseph was chief of one of these smaller bands of Nez Perce. **Back in 1836, Old Joseph had met the Reverend Henry Spalding**. He listened to the missionary and heard the stories of the white man's Book of Heaven. **Old Joseph was one of the Reverend Spalding's first converts.**

The **first son of Old Joseph was born in April of 1840** and given the Indian name, *Hin-may-too-yah-lat-kekht*, which means **Thunder Rolling in the Mountains. He was called Young Joseph**. Two years later, his little brother, Ollikut, was born. **The Reverend Spalding baptized Young Joseph.**

The white man drew up treaties for the chiefs of different tribes to sign. Many promises were made to the Indians. **Almost without exception, the treaties were broken (almost always by the white man).**

Old Joseph moved his band of Nez Perce south to their ancestral home in and around the **Wallowa Valley** where they became known as the **Lower Nez Perce.**

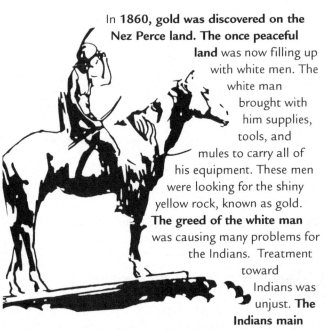

In **1860, gold was discovered on the Nez Perce land. The once peaceful land** was now filling up with white men. The white man brought with him supplies, tools, and mules to carry all of his equipment. These men were looking for the shiny yellow rock, known as gold. **The greed of the white man** was causing many problems for the Indians. Treatment toward Indians was unjust. **The Indians main complaint was against the Indian Bureau, the territorial officials, and the white man's courts.** Indians received stiff punishment for minor misdemeanors, while the white man could kill an Indian in view of other Indians and escape prosecution because no white man witnessed the killing.

In 1863, the United States government wrote another treaty. Eight years earlier in 1855, the government had reduced the Nez Perce land to just 10,000 square miles of reservation land. Now they wanted more land. The white man wanted the Nez Perce to reduce their tribal holding from **10,000 square miles to a little more than 1,000 square miles**. Old Joseph believed that the land was not large enough for all the Indians. **He and his band refused to sign the treaty.**

In 1871, the heavy burden of being chief then fell to Young Joseph. **As his father lay dying, Old Joseph said to his son, "Don't ever sell the bones of your ancestors."** Young Joseph was now Chief Joseph.

FILL IN THE BLANKS:

1. What was the old tribal name for the Nez Perce Indians? _____.

2. In 1836 Old a. _____ met the Reverend b._____ _____.

3. The first son of Old Joseph was given the Indian name of _____ _____ _____ _____ _____ _____.

4. The name means _____ _____ ____ _____ _____.

5. What were the dying words of Old Joseph?

_____

_____

_____."

There was strong pressure from the government to enforce the old treaties, remove the Indians to the reservations, and open the Wallowa Valley to the white settlers. **In 1876 President Ulysses S. Grant ordered General O.O. Howard, Commander of the Northwest Armies, to enforce the treaties.**

A council was called. General Howard would meet with all the Nez Perce Indians at Lapwai, in 1877. General Howard offered Chief Joseph reservation land on the Clearwater located in present day Idaho, and gave the Nez Perce just 30 days to move out of the Wallowa Valley.

Chief Joseph was a great man of peace. Chief Joseph had the gifted ability to be an amazing warfare tactician. He asked for an extension for his people. General Howard said, "No." The Indians had 30 days to leave, and anything left behind would belong to the white men, including livestock.

Chief Joseph had to do what General Howard ordered, but when he returned to his village, he found soldiers were already there. The 30 days had not yet passed. They had to hurry. There was no time to gather all the livestock, and many of the cattle and horses had to be left behind.

Many of the young men of the tribe were angry. They did not want to leave. The young men wanted to stay and fight the white man for their land. Chief Joseph persuaded them to start the journey northward. **The tribe stopped at White Bird Creek to rest.** At this time the angry young men slipped away from the rest camp and attacked and **killed four white settlers.**

The Nez Perce war was now official. The army attacked the tribe at the junction of White Bird Creek and the Salmon River, at White Bird Canyon. The Nez Perce won this battle. Thus began one of the most remarkable retreats in military history.

FILL IN THE BLANKS:

1. In 1876 President a._____ _____ _____ ordered General b.__ __ _____ to enforce the orders for the Indians to move out of   the c. _____ valley.

2. Chief a._____ was a man of b._____.

3. The army had given the Nez Perce just _____days to leave their land.

4. The army attacked the tribe at _____ _____ _____.

5. The _____ _____ won this first battle.

Chief Joseph

Chief Joseph knew that he had no chance of winning a war against the whites. They would head for **Canada, to the "Grandmother's land" and join Chief Sitting Bull and the Sioux Indians.**

Joseph headed for Canada with less than 200 men, many were too old to fight. He also had 600 women and children. His escape plan was to get as many survivors as he could to the Grandmother's land. This retreat extended over 1,300 miles of rugged mountain terrain.

During the retreat, **five battles took place after White Bird Canyon.** Chief Joseph lost only one of these battles.

As the Nez Perce trudged along the **Lolo Trail in the Bitterroot Mountains** they came to a hastily built stockade, where soldiers blocked their path. Other chiefs had joined with Chief Joseph and would go, under a white flag of truce, to talk to the soldiers. These chiefs were **Chief Looking Glass, Chief White Bird, and Chief Too-hool-hool-zote.**

The soldiers were told that the Nez Perce wanted to go to the Crow Indian Nation and wanted to pass through the valley in peace. The Nez Perce were allowed to pass. They passed the stockade, which was to come down through history with the name of **Fort Fizzle.**

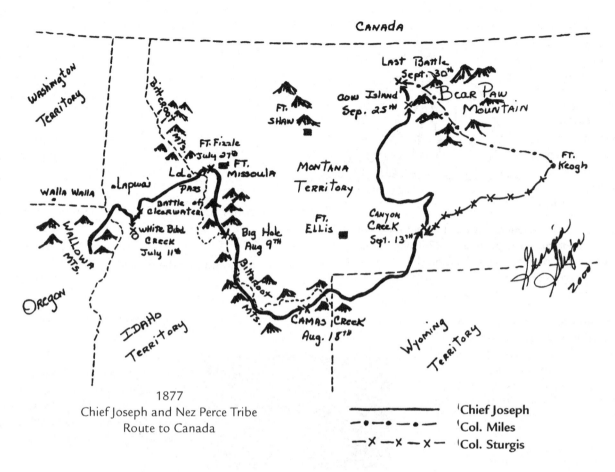

CANADA

Washington Territory

Bitterroot Mts.

Last Battle Sept. 30th

Cow Island Sep. 25th

Bear Paw Mountain

FT. SHAW

FT. Keogh

FT. Fizzle July 27th

FT. Missoula

Lolo Pass

Montana Territory

Lapwai

Walla Walla

Battle of Clearwater

White Bird Creek July 11th

Wallowa Mts.

Big Hole Aug. 9th

FT. Ellis

Canyon Creek Sept. 13th

Oregon

Bitterroot Mts.

IDAHO Territory

Camas Creek Aug. 18th

Wyoming Territory

1877
Chief Joseph and Nez Perce Tribe
Route to Canada

——————— 'Chief Joseph
— • — • — • — 'Col. Miles
— X — X — X — 'Col. Sturgis

On the map use <u>red</u> pen or crayon to trace Chief Joseph's retreat toward Canada, <u>green</u> pen or crayon to follow the route of Colonel Miles, and <u>yellow</u> pen for the route of Colonel Sturgis.

Chief Joseph, the other chiefs, the men, and the non-combatants continued on. Many mountain ranges were crossed, many streams forded by this strange band of old men, young and old women, and children. Still they pushed on, trying to reach the Grandmother's Land and peace.

General Howard was behind them along with the ever-present threat of capture and life on a reservation. From **early August through September** they traveled, the old men, the women, and the children.

On September 13th, 1877, the Indians used an old trick on Colonel Sturgis. The Indians allowed the Colonel and his 7th Cavalry to see them seemingly start toward the Shoshone River. Then the tribe doubled back under cover and cut behind the Colonel and his men. The Indians pushed on toward the Yellowstone River. Colonel Sturgis was hopping mad when he found out he had been outfoxed by Chief Joseph.

General Howard was nearly desperate when he learned that the Nez Perce had escaped from Colonel Sturgis. He would

have to answer to his superiors for letting months pass without the capture of Chief Joseph and his people. **General Howard sent a message to Colonel Nelson Miles, at Fort Keogh on the Tongue River.** He told Miles to move all his available troops northward to intercept the route being taken by the Nez Perce Indians.

At the end of September, the Nez Perce came out of the rugged mountains and made camp on the **Snake Creek near the Bear Paw Mountains**. They had traveled more that **1,600 mile**s and now were **within 40 miles of the Canadian border**. They were tired and many were sick. The Council chiefs decided to make camp. They would camp just long enough to kill some buffalo to provide the needed nourishing food and warm robes. They felt safe because General Howard was several days' march behind them. They did not know that at that very minute Colonel Miles and his troops were bearing down on them.

On September 30th, 1877, the last battle of the Nez Perce tribe was fought. Many of the Indians were killed. The Nez Perce fought bravely, but the cold weather, lack of proper food, and lack of rest had taken their toll.

Chief Joseph's brother, Ollikut, was killed along with Too-hool-hool-zote. The battle ended on October 4th, 1877, as General Howard reached the battlefield. The last to die was Chief Looking Glass.

The Nez Perce war was now over. Chief Joseph stood before General Howard. Chief Joseph draped a blanket about himself and, with quiet pride, handed over his rifle to Colonel Nelson Miles. Before a translator and a recording officer, **Joseph spoke these words:**

"Tell General Howard I know his heart. What he told me before I have in my heart. I am tired of fighting. Our chiefs are killed. Looking Glass is dead. The old men are all killed. It is the young men who say yes or no. He who led the young men is dead. It is cold and we have no blankets. The little children are freezing to death. My people, some of them, have run away to the hills and have no blankets, no food; no one knows where they are, perhaps they are freezing to death. I want time to look for my children and see how many of them I can find. Maybe I shall find them among the dead. Hear me, my chiefs, I am tired; my heart is sick and sad. From where the sun now stands, I will fight no more, forever."

The Nez Perce Indians were never allowed to return to their beloved valley in the Wallowa Mountains. Joseph and his people were loaded onto a riverboat and sent down the Missouri River toward Fort Abraham Lincoln in Dakota Territory, where they expected to spend the winter. **But while they were on the riverboat, the promise that Colonel Miles and General Howard had made to them was overruled by General Sherman. The promise was that the Nez Perce would be allowed to return to their Wallowa Valley.** Instead they were sent to Fort Leavenworth, Kansas, then to the Indian Territory in what is now Oklahoma.

Finally, in 1885, the remaining Nez Perce tribe was sent to the Colville Reservation in Washington Territory.

On September 21, 1904 Chief Joseph died. The reservation doctor said he had died of a broken heart. The death of this great man signaled the end of a great nation and the end of an era.

FILL IN THE BLANKS:

1. The Nez Perce would head for Canada, to the

   _____ _____.

2. They would join up with a._____ _____

   and his b._____Indians.

3. The retreat extended over some _____ miles.

4. During the retreat there were a. _____ battles that

   took place after White b. _____ _____.

5. The last Nez Perce War was fought on _____

   _____ _____.

6. Chief Joseph's brother _____ was killed.

7. The battle ended on October 4th, _____.

8. Chief Joseph handed his weapon to Colonel Nelson

   _____.

9. Write out the last words of Chief Joseph's speech:

   "From where

   _____

   _____

   _____."

Railroads

In the late 1800s, there were many ways for men to travel from one part of the country to another. On water they could use canoes, rafts, ferries, steamboats, or large clipper ships. On land they could walk or ride a horse or mule. There were wagons, stagecoaches, and just about anything you could sit on or put wheels on to carry men from one destination to another.

The era of the railroads was coming to Oregon. There are many stories about men who came to Oregon to build railroads and get rich. We will look at what happened to four men.

BEN HOLLADAY

In the early 1860s, Ben Holladay had almost complete control over the stagecoaches running between the Missouri frontier crossing to California. He had a few pony-express lines, as well, but he sold them to Wells, Fargo & Company. Holladay made a lot of money and bought a line of steamships running from San Francisco, California to Portland, Oregon.

In Portland there were men who believed that a railroad line from Portland into California would allow them to ship lumber and grain into California. Then this shipment would be put on another railroad line and shipped to the East. That other railroad line was the famous Union Pacific.

These men could not agree as to where to build this new railroad. Some of the men wanted the tracks laid down on the western side of the Willamette River. The others wanted the railroad on the east side of the Willamette River. With all the arguing, they were called the "**West Siders**" and the "**East Siders**."

Ben Holladay came to Portland in 1868 and became the leading man for the East Siders. After bitter struggles between both sides, it was decided that the first group to finish 20 miles of track would be declared the victor. The victor would be awarded the land grant, which the U.S. government had promised. The East Siders won, and Ben Holladay got busy building a railroad.

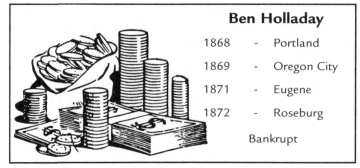

Ben Holladay

1868	-	Portland
1869	-	Oregon City
1871	-	Eugene
1872	-	Roseburg
		Bankrupt

Holladay started in the fall of 1869. He had laid the twenty miles of track to about six miles south of Oregon City by December 23, 1869.

By 1871, he had trains running between Portland and Eugene. In 1872, the train arrived in Roseburg, Oregon. Holladay had spent most of his own money and a great deal of other peoples' money. When hard financial times swept over the country in **1873, the Holladay railroad went bankrupt**. Holladay was broke.

FILL IN THE BLANKS:

1. In the early 1860s _____ _____ had almost complete control over the stagecoaches.

2. The a. "_____ _____" won and Ben Holladay got busy building a

   b. _____.

3. By 1871 he had trains running between

   a. _____ and

   b. _____.

4. By a. _____ the trains arrived in

   b. _____.

HENRY VILLARD

Henry Villard now arrived on the scene. Henry was an American of German descent. When Holladay went bankrupt, a group of wealthy German businessmen bought 11 million dollars' worth of Holladay's railroad bonds.

The German businessmen put Henry Villard in charge. Henry believed, as did Ben Holladay, that the railroads in the Pacific Northwest would become an empire.

In 1881, Mr. Villard organized the Oregon and California Railroad. He got started building tracks south from Roseburg. Ashland, Oregon, was reached in 1884. In 1884 Henry Villard went bankrupt. People were not so quick to adapt to the railroads, wagons and stage coaches

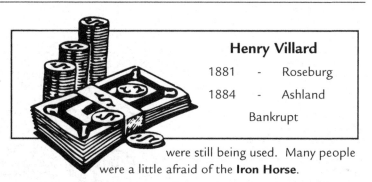

Henry Villard

1881	-	Roseburg
1884	-	Ashland
		Bankrupt

were still being used. Many people were a little afraid of the **Iron Horse**.

The railroad did go on to cross the Siskiyou Mountains and to connect with a railroad from San Francisco in 1887.

Holladay had built 200 miles of railroad track in Oregon. **Villard had built 700 miles of track**. Yes, railroads were definitely becoming very important to our country and to

Oregon. **Seven days were needed for a stagecoach trip** between Portland, Oregon and Sacramento, California. A **steam locomotive engine required only 38 hours**. Yes, the railroads were becoming important as a mode of transportation.

For several years railroad building went on more quietly. Then Hill and Harriman came on the scene.

FILL IN THE BLANKS:

1. In 1881 Mr. Villard organized the Oregon and _____ Railroad.

2. In 1884 _____ was reached.

3. Holladay built _____ miles of track and Villard built _____ miles of track.

4. It took a stagecoach _____ days to travel from Portland to Sacramento.

5. A steam engine could make the trip in _____ hours.

Using your dictionary, define the following:

1. **interpreter**

_____

_____

_____.

2. **treaty**

_____

_____

_____.

3. **retreat**

_____

_____

_____.

4. **escape**

_____

_____

_____.

5. **Indian reservation**

_____

_____

_____.

6. **stockade**

_____

_____

_____.

7. **tactic**

_____

_____

_____.

8. **bankrupt**

_____

_____

_____.

9. **elected**

_____

_____

_____.

THE LAST RAILROAD BATTLE IN OREGON
HILL vs. HARRIMAN

James J. Hill built a railroad in Washington, from Spokane to Seattle, going by way of the northern bank of the Columbia River. The railroad crossed the Columbia River and stopped in Portland. On March 11, 1890, the rails were completed and the line became known as the Spokane, Portland, and Seattle Railroad Company. From 1905 to 1908, Hill continued to build.

Hill was not satisfied with what he had; he wanted to lay more track. He had an idea to build a line **southward from the Columbia River by way of the Deschutes Canyon, through Central Oregon**. This way the farmers and cattlemen of the high desert would not have to go all the way across the Cascades to take advantage of a railroad. It would be right there for them.

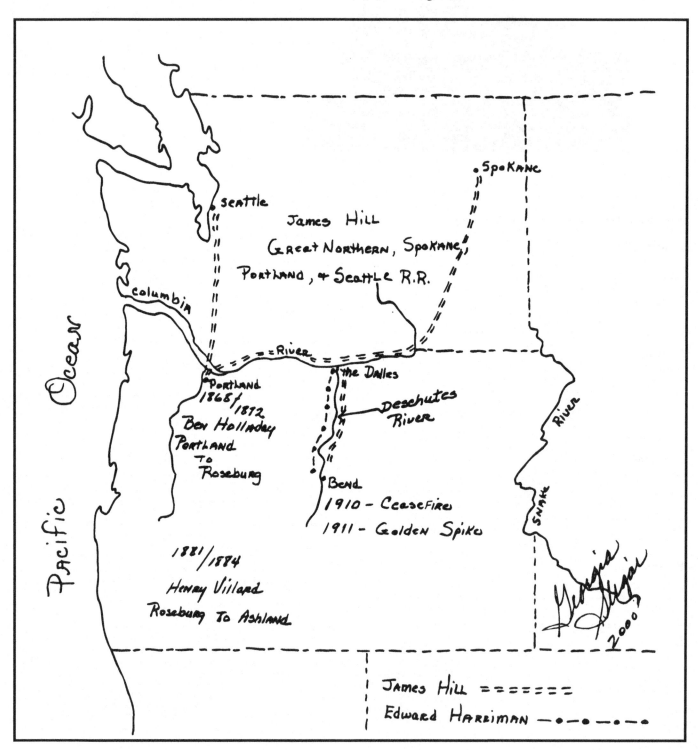

Hill sent his engineers into the Deschutes River area disguised as fisherman. They had orders to buy the land from the farmers. If the farmers knew that their land was wanted for a railroad, they would raise the price of the land.

Hill was interested in the east side of the Deschutes River. When **Edward H. Harriman heard about Hill's plans in midsummer of 1909,** he announced that he would build a railroad along the west bank. It was like a red flag being waved in the face of James Hill. **The Railroad War was on**.

FILL IN THE BLANKS:

1. On March 11, a. _____,

   Hill's railroad line was completed and became known as

   the b._____, _____, and

   _____ _____

   _____.

2. Hill sent his a._____ into the Deschutes River

   area disguised as b._____.

3. Hill was interested in the _____ side of the river.

4. Harriman would build a railroad along the

   _____ side of the river.

Hill and Harriman started their crews up the canyon of the Deschutes. Track was laid on one side of the canyon by Hill's men. Harriman's men laid track on the other side. The workers could watch each other and gauge the progress on the other side.

There were casual gun battles. Bullets flew from one side of the canyon to the other. Supplies were brought in from The Dalles. Late at night some of the men from one side would cross the river and move the supplies. In the morning things would be missing. The men were so close in some places they could throw rocks at each other.

Sometimes it got a lot worse. When a day's work was done, a gang from one camp would cross over to the other camp for a knockdown, drag-out fight. **Even the dynamite was not safe**. Some evenings men would cross the river, find the dynamite shed, and set off the explosives. Men died and those who lived were often maimed. **Yet no charges of murder or assault were filed. The men seemed**

to consider personal injury as just another hazard of the railroad building business.

The building of a railroad was not to be taken lightly. It was hard, backbreaking work. Because European and Chinese immigrants would work hard for little pay, they were hired. **The Chinese especially were hard workers. On the job they earned from 20 to 30 cents per hour**. They worked from early morning, before sunrise, to well after dark. They worked not only with the pick ax and shovel, but also at cooking and keeping the camp running smoothly.

The war along the Deschutes had reached a peak that could not last. Many millions of dollars had been poured into the battle **because of the pride of two men, Hill and Harriman**. Neither man wanted to admit defeat. They were like tired old warriors. At last they realized that all of this was a personal war and that each had wanted to be the top man. The railroad battle was a result of their pride.

From your Bible, write out these Scriptures below:

Proverbs 29:23 _____

_____

_____

_____

_____.

Proverbs 16:18_____

_____

_____

_____

_____.

A cease-fire agreement was reached on May 17, 1910. The two men, James J. Hill and Edward H. Harriman, decided to share the rails for eleven miles and later the joint use was extended.

The golden spike, or last spike, to hold the last rail was driven in Bend on October 5, 1911, two years after the battle started. The battle was over and central Oregon had a railroad in its front yard.

By now the automobile had made its way to Oregon. It is recorded that in 1905 there were 218 automobiles in the state. A new age had begun, the age of fast travel. Just 100 years after Lewis and Clark had trudged down the banks of the Columbia River and built Fort Clatsop, the automobile was now making that same trip, but much faster.

FILL IN THE BLANKS:

1. The men building the tracks across the Deschutes were

   so close they could throw _____ at each other.

2. No charges of a._____ or b._____

   were filed.

3. The men seemed to consider personal injury as just

   another _____

   _____.

4. The _____ were especially hard workers.

5. On the job they earned from _____ to _____ cents

   per hour.

6. Many millions of dollars were poured into the battle

   because of the _____ of two men.

7. A a._____-_____ agreement was

   reached on May 17, b._____.

8. The _____ spike was driven in _____.

9. In 1905 there were _____ automobiles in Oregon.

The Determined Lady Wins

The right to vote: now there's a subject to make hair bristle. Only men could vote! The fight for the right for women to be able to vote was a long, often uphill battle. On the national level we are familiar with **Susan B. Anthony**. What about Oregon? Who would step forward in Oregon to battle for the right for women to vote?

Write out the definition for:

suffrage

_____
_____
_____
_____
_____
_____
_____.

The tough little lady who won the hearts and respect of the people of Oregon was Abigail Scott Duniway.

Abigail Scott traveled across the plains on the 1852 wagon train with her family. On the trail she watched as first her mother and later a younger brother died. They were buried beside the trail.

A year after arriving in Oregon, **Abigail married Benjamin C. Duniway**. She settled down to be a housewife and mother. She did not see her role as anything else until an accident injured her husband. Abigail then had to be the one to provide for the family. They moved to Albany, Oregon, and Abigail opened a millinery (hats) and notions store. The store proved to be a success, but a greater calling was in store for Abigail.

In 1871 the family moved to Portland. The battle was launched! Abigail would fight the fight for freedom for women to be able to vote. Women would not be second-class citizens anymore – not if Abigail could help it!

Abigail started her own newspaper, *The New Northwest.* **It was a weekly newspaper that ran from 1871 to 1887.**

Many times eggs and tomatoes were thrown at her as she spoke to groups of people. Some people thought she was a troublemaker. They liked the world the way it was and didn't want to see changes or progress. But change was coming!

Mrs. Duniway's brother, Harvey W. Scott, did not support his sister's views. Harvey Scott was the editor of *The Oregonian*, **a newspaper that opposed women's suffrage and Abigail's efforts.**

As a speaker, Abigail was witty, quick to sense and feel the mood of the people. She was a gifted speaker with many down-to-earth stories to relate. She was a tireless woman. Despite all her meetings and speeches she still raised a daughter and five sons.

Finally, after all her hard work, women were given the VOTE! **In 1912, in Oregon, women were given the right to vote**. All the hard work had paid off. This was a beginning, a new beginning.

Abigail Scott Duniway died three years later in October 1915, just days short of being 81 years old. She was a tough, determined little lady.

FILL IN THE BLANKS:

1. Only _____ could vote.

2. Suffrage means:

   _____

   _____

   _____

   _____.

3. Abigail a. _____came across the

   plains on a wagon train in the year b. _____ .

4. Abigail married _____.

5. Abigail started her own _____.

6. The name of the newspaper was _____ _____

   _____.

7. Harvey Scott was the editor of _____

   _____.

8. Abigail raised a._____ daughter and b._____ sons.

9. In a. _____ women were given the right to

   b. _____.

A LADY STARTS A COLLEGE

Many women have become important to the history of our country and our state. One such woman was **Tabitha Brown**.

Tabitha Brown came to Oregon with the wagon train in 1846. Accompanying her was her brother-in-law, 77-year-old Captain John Brown. Tabitha's son Orus and his family were also on the wagon train.

The wagon train split at Fort Hall. The party that Tabitha traveled with joined the train that was to take the new, easier southerly route. They were to find out that it was not an easier route. They suffered many hazards and difficulties. The mountains were rugged.

They endured threats from the local Indians. Many of the wagons broke down and the food was all but gone.

They finally found themselves all alone. Near the site of present-day Roseburg, the wagons gave out completely. The days were cold and the nights were even colder. The horses were close to dying. After many hardships and near mishaps, they finally arrived in Salem on Christmas day 1846, with just the clothes on their backs.

Tabitha found a small coin called a *picayune*, worth about six cents, in the finger of her glove. She was able to purchase enough buckskin with the money to make gloves that she sold to the ladies of Salem. She continued to work very hard and wanted to see a dream fulfilled. **She wanted to start a school for the children of the area. She wanted to see the children taught the three Rs (reading, writing, and arithmetic).**

Tabitha started a small school for orphans at West Tualatin Plains, known today as Forest Grove. The school began to prosper. The school was known as **Tualatin Academy but now is known by the name of Pacific University.** A building at the university honors Tabitha Brown. The building was named after her.

There are many women who are famous. We have looked at just a few of them:

· **Anna Maria Pittman Lee**,
   wife of the Reverend Jason Lee
· **Narcissa Prentiss Whitman**,
   wife of Dr. Marcus Whitman
· **Eliza Spalding**,
   wife of the Reverend Henry H. Spalding
· **Abigail Scott Duniway**
· **Tabitha Brown**

FILL IN THE BLANKS:

1. Tabitha Brown came to Oregon in _____.

2. The wagon train split at _____ _____.

3. The finally arrived at a. _____ on

   b. _____ day 1846.

4. Tabitha found a small a. _____ called a

   b. _____ in the finger of a glove.

5. It was worth about _____ cents.

6. She wanted to start a _____.

7. She wanted the children to learn the three Rs

   a._____   b._____ and

   c. _____.

8. The school she started, known as Tualatin Academy, is

   today known as _____ _____.

Our State Government

Each and every state has a government that is patterned after the government of the United States.

Sixty delegates chosen by the people, drew up our Oregon Constitution. They met August to September, 1857. On November 9, 1857, the Constitution was approved by the vote of the people of Oregon Territory. **When Oregon became a state on February 14, 1859**, the Constitution became official. The Constitution divides the work of the state government into three parts or branches.

I   **Legislative Branch**

II   **Executive Branch**

III   **Judicial Branch**

Let us take a look at each Branch.

LEGISLATIVE BRANCH

The legislative branch has two parts:

1.   **Senate**
2.   **House of Representatives**

These two bodies of state government make laws for our state. **To serve in either the Senate or House of Representatives you must be 21 years old, a citizen of the United States, and have lived in Oregon at least three years.** Those elected to the Senate serve four years and may be re-elected. Oregon elects 30 state senators.

There are 60 members of the state House of Representatives. They each serve a two-year term and may be re-elected.

When both the state Senate and state House of Representatives agree on a bill or law, they then send it to the governor.

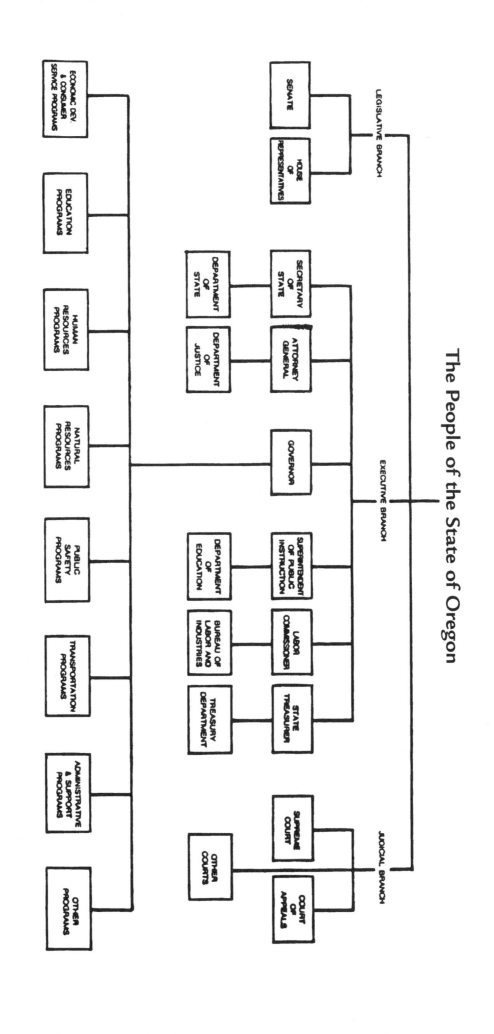

The People of the State of Oregon

FILL IN THE BLANKS:

1. Oregon became a state on _____ ____ _____.

2. Name the three branches of our state government.

    a._____

    b._____

    c._____

3. Name the two parts of the Legislative Branch.

    a._____

    b._____

4. To serve in either the Senate or House of

   Representatives you must be:

    a. _____ years old.

    b. A_____ of the United States and have lived

   in Oregon for c. _____years.

5. The State Senator serves a term of a. _____ years and

   a state Representative in the House of Representatives

   serves a term of b. _____ years.

EXECUTIVE BRANCH

To be our governor you must be at least 30 years old, a citizen of the United States, and a resident of Oregon for three years. The governor is limited to two terms in office.

Example:

1998-2002—-4 years

2002-2006—-4 years

The governor is our chief executive, meaning he is in charge. He prepares the state budget and determines how much money will be spent on state projects. **He is commander-in-chief of our state's military forces. The governor has the power to veto a bill sent from the Senate and House of Representatives.**

Define the term: Veto

_____

_____

_____

_____

_____.

The governor also appoints many people to be in charge of agencies, boards, and commissions. The governor and the executive branch of our government sees that our laws are carried out.

Some of the top elected posts in Oregon government are:

a. Governor   d. Secretary of State

b. State Treasurer   e. Labor Commissioner

c. Attorney General

The governor provides leadership, planning, and coordination for the executive branch of state government. He appoints many department and agency heads within the executive branch and appoints members to more than 200 policymaking, regulatory and advisory boards, and commissions.

If the office of the governor ever becomes vacant, the office passes, in order, to the:

1. Secretary of State

2. State Treasurer

3. President of the Senate

4. Speaker of the House of Representatives

The governor appoints judges to fill vacancies in judicial office. He has authority to grant reprieves, commutations and pardons of criminal sentences.

FILL IN THE BLANKS:

1. To be governor you must be:

    a. _____ years old

    b. A _____ of the United States and have lived

   in Oregon for c. _____ years.

2. The governor is our _____ ____ _____.

3. The governor has the power to _____ a bill.

4. Some of the elected posts are:

    a. _____

    b. _____

    c. _____

    d. _____

    e. _____

JUDICIAL BRANCH

The judicial branch consists of the state Supreme Court, the Court of Appeals, and many other lesser courts. These courts settle arguments and determine punishments for crimes.

INITIATIVE AND REFERENDUM

Mr. William S. U'Ren was the first to bring the initiative and referendum process to Oregon. Mr. U'Ren came to Oregon in 1890. He came wanting to help people govern themselves and to avoid corruption in government. Mr. U'Ren was advised that if he wanted to really help the people, he should work not as president or even as a chairman, but go to work behind the scenes to change the government into a good government.

The initiative and referendum were first used extensively in Switzerland. Just what are the Initiative and the Referendum? Essentially they are simple to understand. **Initiative makes it possible for people to make laws**, whether or not their elected representatives approve of those laws. **Referendum makes it possible for the people to repeal laws** whether or not elected representatives approve. So it is easy to see that the **Initiative and Referendum could be said to be the "starting and stopping" of laws.**

William U'Ren also brought the Australian, or secret, ballot to Oregon. In 1894, the moment of truth arrived with the vote in both houses of legislature, the Senate and the House of Representatives, against the I & R. It lost by one vote in each house. **The fight continued and again the I & R came up for a vote. This time it passed. In 1899, the I & R passed the House with votes of 44 to 8, and passed the Senate, 22 to 6. At the next general election in 1902, the people of Oregon approved the I & R process by a margin of 11 to 1.** The Initiative and Referendum were here to stay, along with the Australian, or secret ballot. Oregon was considered a progressive state, and the whole process became known as the Oregon System.

The whole process of government moves down to the individual cities and towns. Most Oregon cities have a mayor and other elected officials. **Some cities hire a city manager** to deal with the problems of growth and planning. **Each city has a municipal judge and a city attorney.**

Some Oregon Indians still have government of their own. One group that has been successful lives on the **Warm Springs Indian Reservation** in central Oregon. These Indians have their own tribal council. The council settles disputes on the reservation. It advises the Indians on business and manages the resort, Kah-Nee-Ta.

The Umatilla and Klamath Indians also have a form of tribal government.

FILL IN THE BLANKS:

1. The judicial branch consists of the:

   a. _____

   b. _____

   c. _____

2. These lesser courts settle arguments and determine _____ for crimes.

3. Who first brought the I & R to Oregon?

   _____.

4. The I & R was first used in what country?

   _____.

5. The I & R could be said to be the

   a. "_____ and

   b. _____" of laws.

6. Most Oregon cities have an elected _____.

7. Some cities hire a city _____.

8. Some Oregon Indians still have a

   _____ of their own.

9. Name three (3) Indian tribes that have some form of their own government.

   a._____

   b._____

   c._____

A WELL-REMEMBERED GOVERNOR

One of the best-remembered governors is Oswald West. **Oswald West was the governor of Oregon from 1911 to 1915. Oswald set aside nearly 400 miles of ocean beach for public use. From the mouth of the Columbia River on the north to the California border on the south, all but a few miles are public beaches.** For this, Oregon and her people are indebted to Oswald West.

West is also remembered because he was governor of Oregon when women won the right to vote. **In 1912**

Governor Oswald West went to the home of Abigail Scott Duniway to receive the proclamation he had asked her to write. **It was a very proud moment for one tough little lady and one very popular governor.**

FILL IN THE BLANKS:

1. One of the best-remembered governors is

   _____.

2. Oswald set aside nearly a._____ miles of ocean beaches

   for b._____ _____.

3. West was the governor of Oregon when women

   won the right to _____.

4. The year was _____.

5. He went to the home of

   _____ to

   receive the proclamation she was

   asked to write.

Governors Of Oregon

1. Provisional Government -- 1843-1848
2. U.S. Territorial Governors -- 1848-1859
3. State Governors -- 1858-Present

1. Provisional Government

First Executive Committee -- 1843-1844
Second Executive Committee -- 1844-1845
George Abernathy -- 1845-1848

2. U.S. Territorial governors

1.	Joseph Lane	Democrat	1848-1850
2.	Kintzing Prichette	Democrat	1850
3.	John P. Gaines	Whig	1850-1853
4.	Joseph Lane	Democrat	1853
5.	George Law Curry	Democrat	1853
6.	John W. Davis	Democrat	1853-1854
7.	George Law Curry	Democrat	1854-1859

3. State Governors

1.	John Whiteaker	Democrat	1859-1862
2.	A.C. Gibbs	Republican	1862-1866
3.	George L. Woods	Republican	1866-1870
4.	La Fayette Grover	Democrat	1870-1877
5.	Stephen F. Chadwick	Democrat	1877-1878
6.	W.W. Thayer	Democrat	1878-1882
7.	Z.F. Moody	Republican	1882-1887
8.	Sylvester Pennoyer	Democrat	1887-1895
9.	William Paine Lord	Republican	1895-1899
10.	T.T. Geer	Republican	1899-1903
11.	George Chamberlain	Democrat	1903-1909
12.	Frank W. Benson	Republican	1909-1910
13.	Jay Bowerman	Republican	1910-1911
14.	Oswald West	Democrat	1911-1915
15.	James Withycombe	Republican	1915-1919
16.	Ben W. Olcott	Republican	1919-1923

17.	Walter M. Pierce	Democrat	1923-1927
18.	I.L. Patterson	Republican	1927-1929
19.	A.W. Norblad	Republican	1929-1931
20.	Julius L. Meier	Independent	1931-1935
21.	Charles H. Martin	Democrat	1935-1939
22.	Charles A. Sprague	Republican	1939-1943
23.	Earl Snell	Republican	1943-1947
24.	John H. Hall	Republican	1947-1949
25.	Douglas McKay	Republican	1949-1952
26.	Paul L. Patterson	Republican	1952-1956
27.	Elmo Smith	Republican	1956-1957
28.	Robert D. Holmes	Democrat	1957-1959
29.	Mark Hatfield	Republican	1959-1967
30.	Tom McCall	Republican	1967-1975
31.	Robert W. Straub	Democrat	1975-1979
32.	Victor G. Atiyeh	Republican	1979-1987
33.	Neil Goldschmidt	Democrat	1987-1991
34.	Barbara Robers	Democrat	1991-1995
35.	John Kitzhaber	Democrat	1995-2003
36.	Ted Kulongoski	Democrat	2003—Incumbent

Select 2 (two) Governors and write a 100 word report.

Information on the above was taken from "Wikipedia.org"

FAMOUS PEOPLE IN OREGON

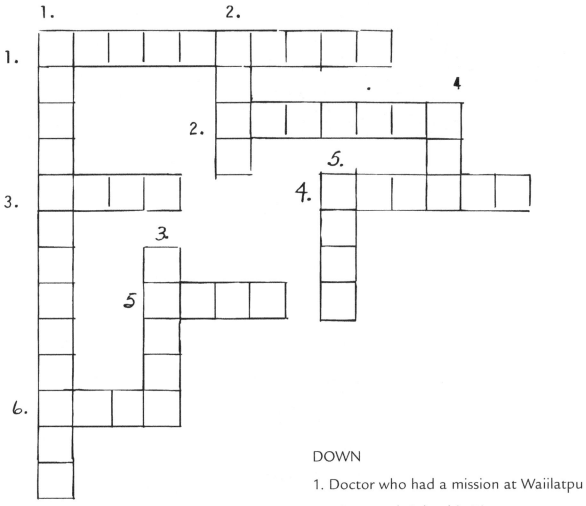

DOWN

1. Doctor who had a mission at Waiilatpu
2. Discovered Columbia River
3. Part of the team with Lewis
4. First Methodist missionary to Oregon
5. Modoc Indian chief

ACROSS

1. Dr. John of Ft. Vancouver
2. Helped women get the vote in Oregon
3. Brought secret ballot to Oregon
4. Nez Perce Indian chief
5. First territorial governor of Oregon
6. Famous mountain man

UNIT V

FILL IN THE BLANKS

1. On February 14,
   a._____, President James
   b. _____
   signed a bill making Oregon the 33rd state of the Union.

2. _____ was the new capital.

3. The old nickname for Portland was _____.

4. The name of the first steamboat built on the Willamette River was the _____.

5. Captain _____ _____ started the Oregon Steam Navigation Co.

6. Name three famous Indian wars.
   a. _____
   b. _____
   c. _____

7. The most famous Modoc Indian was _____ _____.

8. What was the meaning of the name given to the son of Old Joseph?
   "_____ _____ ___ ____
   _____."

9. What were the dying words of Old Joseph?
   "_____ _____ ____ _____ _____
   ___ _____ _____."

10. Ulysses S. Grant ordered General O.O. _____ to enforce the treaties.

11. The army gave the Nez Perce just _____ days to leave their land.

12. The army attacked the tribe at _____ _____ _____.

13. The Nez Perce Indians headed for Canada to what they called the _____ _____.

14. The battle ended on October 4th, 1877, with Chief Joseph handing his rifle to Colonel _____ _____.

15. Write out the final words of Chief Joseph.
    "From where_____
    _____
    _____."

16. Name the two men who fought to build a railroad from the Columbia River, south to and through central Oregon.
    a. _____
    b. _____.

17. _____ _____ _____ was one of the women who helped the women of Oregon to get "The Vote."

18, The little woman who went from one picayune to start what is now Pacific University, was _____ _____.

19. Name the three branches of government.
    a._____
    b._____
    c._____

NOW GO BACK AND STUDY ALL THE QUESTIONS FOR UNIT V TO PREPARE FOR THE FINAL TEST.

Suggested Projects

1. At your local library gather more information on one of the following.
   a. Rogue River War
   b. Modoc War
   c. Captain Jack
   d. Nez Perce War

2. Pick one tribe and write a 250 word report.

3. Build a model railroad. You can use many things including milk cartons, shoe boxes, etc. Use a card table and build a relief area with mountains and valleys and rivers for the trains to run along the riverbed, and show any lava flows in the area.

4. Using the "Famous People in Oregon" as your model, make your own crossword puzzle using people in your family with aunt, uncle, cousin, grandparents, Mom and Dad.

5. Using the "Famous People in Oregon" as your model, make one of your own using towns or cities in your county.

6. If at all possible, visit our state capitol building in Salem, Oregon. Starting at the "grassroots" with your Republican or Democratic Precinct Committee person, find out who represents you in your area, your county, and in our state. Get the names of your state senator, member of the House of Representatives, local mayor or city manager, and others.

Oregon History

STUDENT WORKBOOK

UNIT VI
Land and Animals

- *Plants*
- *Animals*
- *Shipping*

STUDENTS' GOAL	
Target Test Date	_____
Pages in Unit	_____
Pages Per Day	_____
Date Unit Completed	_____
Final Score of Unit	_____

UNIT VI

Land and Animals

To everything there is a season, a time for every purpose under heaven (Ecclesiastes 3:1).

Now read **Ecclesiastes 3:1-8.**

Forests

Shouts could be heard: **fire, fire, fire**! The fire had begun from a very innocent accident. We must go back to **1933**. It was **August 14** and it had been a very hot and dry summer. The driest in many years. The loggers knew that this was the time of year when forest fires start. They were keeping a very sharp eye on the sky. No! There were no clouds in the sky that day. No rain!

A logging camp located on **Gales Creek** had just finished hauling a couple of logs down the trail to be put on a wagon. It was an **accident** — nobody would have done it on purpose. One of the logs was a windfall cedar that was bone-dry and had lain in the forest for years. The log being dragged past was a fir. The **cedar and fir rubbed against each other. The result was a spark. The spark ignited nearby underbrush**.

Today we know that the fire was caused by what every Boy Scout, Girl Scout, Campfire Girl, and 4-H member knows, namely, **fire by friction**.

Within a short time smoke was seen rising above the trees. Because the weather was so dry, the fire could run an awful race. The race was on to see if man could stop the fire before it could do much damage.

The smoke rose to such a height that it could **be seen in Portland, 50 miles away**. The battle continued day and night. Men and more men were sent to fight the fire. **Over 100 men** came the first day to aid the loggers. All the men could see that this was not just a small fire. This was a fire out of control, turning into a **firestorm**.

The fire was so hot that it created its **own high velocity wind**. Hot air rises. As the **hot air rises, it sucks in the cold air at the bottom**, thus causing a firestorm. The fire raced across the forest at **60 to 70 miles per hour**. The tops of trees exploded. There was nothing the men could do but run.

The fire raged for days. The fire **"crowned,"** which meant that it leaped or jumped into the tops of centuries-old **firs as tall as 11 or 12-story buildings**. Still the fire raged. The fire became a towering curtain of flame **15 miles wide, headed toward the ocean.**

Whole tops of trees were carried aloft by the rushing east winds and were blown out to sea with a large amount of ash, most of it still hot. The ash washed back to shore on the incoming tides. For miles along the ocean coast the ash of the **Tillamook Burn** was piled two feet deep.

Finally, when it seemed that all of Oregon's western woodland might be ravaged by flames, a cool, moist blanket of **fog came in from the ocean. The fog drove the fire out of the treetops toward the ground**. The worst of the fire was over. Now the loggers and men who came to help could begin to dig fire lines and put the fire out.

The fire had raged for a couple of weeks and much damage had been done. More than **311,000 acres had burned**, mainly in Tillamook County. Much timber had been lost. **Douglas fir trees that had grown for over 400 years were destroyed**. Now the main job of the men was to clear out the burned logs and debris before another enemy, wood-eating insects, could attack the forest.

The amount of timber burned was estimated to be 12 and a half billion board feet. This is a large figure, but look at it this way. The destroyed lumber was enough to rebuild all the houses built in the United States in 1933.

FILL IN THE BLANKS:

1. The fire began on a. _____ 14, b. _____ .

2. Today we know the fire was caused by

   _____ .

3. The smoke could be seen in a. _____,

   which was about b. _____ miles away.

4. The fire was so hot it created its own _____

   _____ wind.

5. The fire raced across the forest at a. _____ to

   b. _____ miles per hour.

6. The fire a. _____, which meant that it

   b. _____ or c. _____

   into the tops of the trees.

7. What came off the ocean that drove the fire from the

   tops of the trees? _____ .

8. About how many acres were burned?   _____

9. What name has been given to this great fire?

   _____ _____ .

HELP IS ON THE WAY

Good did come out of the **Tillamook Burn**. Oregonians were awakened to the fact that we must protect our forests. We found out that we **must protect our forests not only from natural enemies, but from the most dangerous of all, man and his carelessness.**

Oregon started a program to reforest the burned-out areas. Many **new trees were planted by the schoolchildren of Oregon**. We now have a **"Keep Oregon Green Association"** to help educate people on how to be careful with our forests. If you were to drive with your parents toward **Tillamook from Portland on Highway 6**, you

would see that much of the burn can still be seen. However, many trees have been planted and are growing to cover the scars of the past.

MODERN FIREFIGHTING

New methods of fighting fires are used today. The **airplane** is one method. **Smoke jumpers** are another. Many planes are used today with **tanks filled with chemicals or water** that smother the fire. These planes fly over a fire and drop their load.

Smoke jumpers are flown into an area and dropped from the plane with a parachute. They land near the fire and begin to **dig a firebreak**, or trench, across which they hope the fire will not jump.

OREGON'S PRIME TIMBER

Oregon's prime timber area is divided into two parts. The **Douglas fir region lies west** of the Cascade Mountains. The **ponderosa pine region lies east of the mountains**. We do have other types of trees but the two most famous are the Douglas fir and the ponderosa pine. The Douglas fir was named after the pioneer botanist, David Douglas. He was the first to discover the fir tree.

In 1964, the Goodyear Aerospace Company designed and built a huge triangular balloon, filled with helium. They tried to use it to carry logs out of the forests where it was hard for a truck to go. It worked, and the loggers began to move the logs out of the forest by **hooking the logs to a steel cable that hung down from the balloon**. The Goodyear Company called them *vee-balloons*. Today logging companies do not use the vee-balloons. They still prefer to build roads into the forest and haul the logs out by truck.

To learn more about recent timber laws go to your local library or look in the *Oregon Blue Book*.

In the past we have had many means of transporting our lumber to the mills. **Once we used teams of oxen** to drag the logs to the mill, or to the nearest stream to be floated to the mill. Then we had a network of **small railroads** that would haul the logs to the city and the mill. Now we have **very large trucks** that are loaded with logs. If you pass one on a narrow road, be sure to move out of its way and give the driver plenty of room. He will be in a hurry, and he is much bigger than you.

FILL IN THE BLANKS:

1. The most dangerous enemy to our forests is

    a. _____ and his

    b._____.

2. The Douglas fir region is

    a. _____ of the Cascade Mountains and the ponderosa pine is

    b. _____ of the mountains.

3. Douglas fir was named after _____ _____.

4. In 1964 the

    a. _____ _____ company designed and built a huge

    b. _____ balloon.

5. Name three ways of moving logs to a mill:

    a. _____ teams

    b. small _____

    c. large _____.

The lumber industry is far more efficient today than it was in the beginning. We have learned much about trees and forests. **We now have highly specialized machinery and techniques to make the best use of the trees that we take from our forests.**

The lumber industry employs many thousands of people. Men are still needed to cut the trees down, saw them into logs, transport the logs to lumber mills, operate the lumber mills, and market the lumber products.

In the early days, products made from Northwestern lumber were **almost entirely used for construction.** Today other major industries are based on forest resources. The **manufacture of wood pulp and paper** is just one of them.

All paper is made from the cellulose fiber of plants and trees. Early mills obtained this fiber from straw and rags. Later, they began using such woods as **cottonwood, fir, hemlock, and spruce.** Today, leading pulpwood trees in the Pacific Northwest include **western hemlock, Douglas fir, lodgepole pine, silver fir, white fir, and sitka spruce.** In recent years, improved methods have made it possible to use sawmill waste in the manufacture of pulp, as well as certain hardwood species.

Before the cellulose fiber in the wood can be extracted, the wood must first be turned into a pulp. There are **two general methods** for doing this.

First, by mechanical processes, the log is forced against a powerful grindstone, which grinds it into a fine pulp. This kind of pulp is called **groundwood pulp.** It is used for cheap grades of paper, such as newsprint. **The second method is a chemical process.** The wood is chipped, then cooked in a special chemical solution, which breaks down the fibers. After the wood is reduced to a pulp, it is necessary to separate the wood fibers from the pulp. There are various processes, which may include **sifting, beating, fluffing, washing, and drying.** The fibers are then matted together into a felt, and the final product begins to take shape. After the

SAWMILL

felt goes through various pressing and drying processes, it becomes paper.

The plywood industry has grown tremendously since World War II. The Northwest's major resource in the plywood industry is the Douglas fir. More than half the plywood produced in this country is made from Douglas fir. Logs suitable for plywood are straight, round, free of decay or knots, and the bigger the better.

Big, **first-growth Douglas fir** trees supply the best "**peeler**" logs, as they are called. After the bark is removed, the peeler log is subjected to a steam bath to soften its surface. It is then ready for the rotary lathe, which peels or **unwinds the log into one long strip of veneer**. This strip is sliced into different lengths, called plies or panels. The panels then receive a coating of glue. After the application of glue, the panels are placed against each other, so the grain of one panel runs at right angles to the grain of the panel next to it. **Plywood usually consists of three, five, or seven panels**. After the panels are placed in position, they are subjected to tremendous pressure and heat to glue them securely together.

The reinforcement, provided by the glue and the contrasting direction of the grain in the panels, results in a product of super strength. Plywood has other advantages also. It can be made into wood panels of almost any size. It can be bent and made into curved shapes. Plywood is used in the manufacture of many products, including **flooring, siding for houses, wall paneling, furniture, cabinets for the home, counters**, and forms into which concrete is poured for use on construction projects.

Many, many products come from our forests. **We have learned over the years to use those things that God has put on our earth for us to use and enjoy.**

FILL IN THE BLANKS:

1. In the early days products made from the Pacific Northwest lumber were used almost entirely for

   _____.

2. Paper is made from the _____ _____ of plants and trees.

3. Name four leading trees used to make pulpwood.

   a. _____ b. _____

   c. _____ d. _____

4. Name two processes that make pulp.

   a. _____

   b. _____

5. Big, first-growth

   a. _____ _____ trees supply the best b. _____ logs.

Name five products that plywood is used for:

_____

_____

_____

_____

_____

Using your dictionary, define these words:

1. **friction**

   _____
   _____
   _____ .

2. **botanist**

   _____
   _____
   _____ .

3. **helium**

   _____
   _____
   _____ .

4. **pungent**

   _____
   _____
   _____ .

5. **velocity**

   _____
   _____
   _____ .

Oregon Trees

And out of the ground the Lord God made every tree grow that is pleasant to the sight and good for food. The tree of life was also in the midst of the garden, and the tree of the knowledge of good and evil (Genesis 2:9).

Let us now study some of our Oregon trees. There are **two major kinds of trees in our beautiful state: needleleaf and broadleaf**. Pine and spruce are needleleaf trees. They are called conifers. **Conifer, from the word "cone,"** means that the seeds are in the cones. Conifers are softwoods. All conifers in Oregon, except the larch, are evergreen.

Broadleaf trees such as oak, maple, and alder are not **evergreen**. They are considered **deciduous**. That means they do not stay green all year long. They lose their leaves in the fall. They are also called "**hardwoods**."

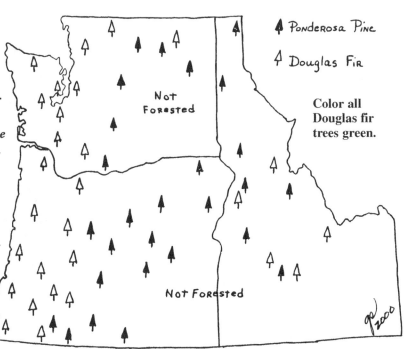

Ponderosa Pine

Douglas Fir

Color all Douglas fir trees green.

Not Forested

Not Forested

DOUGLAS FIR

In 1939, the Oregon legislature named the Douglas fir as Oregon's state tree. For a long time loggers have called it the "**Doug fir.**" The Douglas fir was named in honor of David Douglas, a young **botanist** who came to the **Oregon country in 1825** to discover and describe new kinds of trees, plants, and flowers.

Fir
Cones upward, pulled needles leave no spur

About three-quarters of Oregon's yearly wood crop is Douglas fir. The Doug fir is, next to the redwood or sequoia, the fastest growing conifer. Some grow to a height of 200 feet. The average height at the time of cutting is between 160 and 180 feet. The Douglas fir has cones with tiny, three-pointed bracts. No other tree in Oregon has these "pitchforks."

These bracts sticking out between the cone scales have been described as looking like the hind feet and tail of a mouse disappearing down a hole.

PONDEROSA PINE

The ponderosa pine has long narrow needles bound in little bundles. Each **ponderosa bundle** usually has **three needles from five to ten inches long. The lodgepole pine has two needles in a bundle. The white and sugar pines have bundles with five needles.** Pines grow in the drier parts of Oregon. Their foliage is open compared to that of the fir, spruce, or hemlock. Thus the sun filters through all the way to the forest floor. The pines send roots deep into the earth in search of moisture.

The ponderosa pine is the important conifer east of the Cascades, just as Douglas fir is west of the mountains. Young ponderosas have dark gray to black bark. In **older trees the bark is golden.** The bark consists of large, flat, red to gold plates. About **60 % of central and eastern Oregon's forests are ponderosa pine.** It is Oregon's number two tree. Its straight grain makes good furniture, cabinets, walls, window frames, and doors. Sometimes **ponderosa pines grow over 240 feet tall with trunks as thick as eight to nine feet.**

Pine
Needles in bundles of 2, 3 or 5 enclosed at base in sheath of bud scales

FILL IN THE BLANKS:

1. Name two major kinds of trees in Oregon

   a. _____

   b. _____.

2. Conifer comes from the word _____.

3. In a. _____ (what year) the Oregon legislature

   named the b. _____ as the

   state tree.

4. The loggers gave it the name of _____.

5. The Douglas fir can grow to a height of _____

   feet.

6. The ponderosa pine grows mostly in the _____

   part of the state.

7. In older trees the ponderosa bark is _____.

8. What _____% of central and eastern Oregon's forests

   is ponderosa pine.

WESTERN RED CEDAR

The cedar's leaves are flat and lacy, a bit like a fern. The cedar branch has tiny scales that overlap. The bark from the **cedar tree was used by some Indians to make skirts, capes, and hats**. The wood from the **cedar was used by the coastal Indians to build houses, canoes**, and **cooking bowls. The Indians used the cedar also in making fish nets, ropes, baskets, and mats.**

Western red cedar. Notice how lacy it is.

The wood of western red cedar is light and soft and straight-grained. It has a reddish color and a sweet, clean smell.

The **western red cedar grows very slowly. Douglas fir is ready to cut when 70 years old. Cedar needs 200 to 250 years before it is fully grown**. Old stands of first-growth western red cedar are slowly disappearing. Because it takes cedar so long to grow, it is not being replanted. Soon only in wilderness areas and in national and state parks will you be able to see giant western red cedar.

SITKA SPRUCE

Sitka spruce grows all along the **Oregon Coast**. The trees are very big around (circumference). **They grow as tall as 180 feet**. The needles are stiff and quite sharp. They are single rather than in clusters. Each needle comes out of a tiny platform or pedestal.

The wood of sitka spruce is very lightweight, yet stronger for its weight than any other wood. This makes it useful for making ladders, oars, or airplanes. **During the First World War we needed much sitka spruce in the manufacture of aircraft**. Spruce wood is also very sensitive to sound. That quality is called resonance. **Often pianos, organs, and violins are made from spruce**. Sitka spruce chips make fine newsprint.

Spruce
Cones downward, pulled needles leave spurs on twig

Driving from Portland to Cannon Beach or Seaside on Highway 26, you will pass a sign pointing out the "Largest Sitka Spruce" on the West Coast. It is a joy to behold and well worth the stop to see the tree.

Fill in the answers to the following:

1. Cedar leaves are _____ and lacy.

2. Some Indians used the bark of the cedar for

   (name two) a. _____ b. _____.

3. Cedar needs _____ to 250 years to grow.

4. The sitka spruce can grow as tall as _____ feet.

5. The needles are _____ and quite sharp.

6. During the First World War, sitka spruce was used for

   making _____.

7. Because of the resonance of the spruce wood, they were

   often made into a. _____,

   b. _____, and c. _____.

WESTERN JUNIPER

Throughout eastern Oregon you can see junipers on every side. They take varied and unusual shapes. The **juniper berries are blue**. They are actually cones that never open. The resin inside these **berries gives off a sharp, pungent odor**.

The juniper is a little like a camel. It can live with **less water than any other Oregon tree**. Junipers live longer than most other trees. Like the yew, junipers make fine fence posts. There is an old saying that "one juniper fencepost will outlast two postholes." The dark green color of the juniper stands out against the dry hills and rim rock of the high desert area in central Oregon and eastern Oregon. Juniper and sagebrush give the Oregon desert a spicy smell, especially after a rain.

Juniper
Fruits berrylike, needles in 2s or 3s, spreading or scalelike and tightly overlapping

RED ALDER

The red alder loves water. Few streams in western Oregon are without alders. The alder, the most common broadleaf in Oregon, consists of a small group of trees and shrubs. Oregon has four types of alder.

1. red   2. white   3. mountain   4. black

Alders are part of the birch family. Alders are known for their large, blunt-toothed leaves, and woody cones. The woody cones hang from the trees like tiny lanterns. The trunk is gray-white with black patches. If you chew the inner bark, your saliva and tongue will turn red.

They grow in cool, moist soil that is found in and around the Coast Range in western Oregon. It is not often found east of the Cascades. It **is seldom found above 2,500 feet in elevation**. The red alder is a fast growing tree and can grow to a **height of 60 feet**. It is "old" **at 50 to 60 years of age. The bark is used in dyeing and tanning cloth** and

hides. The wood can be used for bridges and pilings because it resists underwater rot.

The red alder is an important hardwood. It outnumbers all other broadleaf trees in Oregon. This tree is used in paper mills. The red alder is also turned into furniture, cabinets, and toys. The alder supply of Oregon is large and growing.

WHITE ALDER

The less plentiful **white alder grows on both sides of the Cascade Mountains**. It is like the **red alder, but can be grown smaller and then sometimes taller**. In some areas it has been known to grow as tall as 90 feet. Its inner bark does not turn red when peeled.

The mountain alder can grow to be 35 feet tall, and the black alder can grow to 10 feet.

FILL IN THE BLANKS:

1. The resin inside the juniper berry gives off a sharp, _____ odor.

2. Why is the juniper like a camel? _____ _____ _____.

3. Red alder loves _____.

4. The alder is part of the _____ family.

5. The white alder does not turn _____ when the bark is peeled.

Red alder
Notice the small cones

OREGON WHITE OAK

The Oregon **white oak grows mainly west of the Cascade Mountains. Outposts of this tree have been found near The Dalles and south into the Tygh Valley. The white oak can be found in the Siskiyou Mountains and in groves up and down the Willamette Valley. Only now and then does the white oak show up beyond the crest of the Coast Range.**

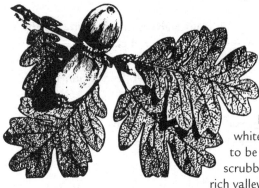

Oregon white oak. Indians ate the acorns

No other oaks of the Pacific Northwest have rounded lobes. In the dry hills, the white oak is likely to be short and scrubby, but on rich valley soil it often grows 60 feet and taller. **In the winter you can see clusters of mistletoe growing in the crowns of the white oak.**

Oregon white oak makes good flooring and furniture. However, it is not used very much because eastern forests meet market needs. Oregon oaks are scattered and their trunks are short. It is hard to get a good, long board out of them.

The **acorns of the white oak were part of the Indian's food supply.** The leaves have nearly as much protein as alfalfa hay. They furnish good browse for the deer. In pioneer days, many Willamette Valley cattle survived a hard winter by eating oak twigs.

BIGLEAF MAPLE

The bigleaf maple is well named. Its leaves are from six to twelve inches across. Sometimes the **leaf measures 15 inches in diameter.** Of all the maple leaves in the world, this is the largest. **It has five lobes and looks a lot like the human hand with the fingers spread wide.**

The bigleaf maple has the largest leaf of all the maples in the world.

Bigleaf maples grow in western Oregon. This common native shade tree in western Oregon likes valleys and foothills. Handsome furniture is made from this tree. Maple burls are used in making veneer.

It is possible to get maple syrup from the bigleaf maple. However, it takes much effort and you don't get much syrup. Our spring nights are not cold enough and our days not hot enough to produce the heavy flow of sap that maples in Vermont give. Squirrels and birds feast in the big tree's shade.

FILL IN THE BLANKS:

1. The white oak grows mainly _____ of the Cascades.

2. In the winter you can see clusters of _____ in the crowns of the white oak.

3. _____ of the white oak were part of the Indians' diet.

4. The leaves of the bigleaf maple can grow from _____ to ____ inches in diameter.

5. The bigleaf maple grows in _____ Oregon.

OREGON MYRTLE

The **Oregon myrtle tree is related to the laurel family.** Californians call it California laurel. We call it "myrtle wood." Oregon myrtle bears yellow, olive-shaped fruit. Its shiny, narrow, leathery leaves smell of camphor when crushed. Hudson's Bay Company men brewed tea from myrtle leaves for treating a chill.

Myrtle wood is well known in gift shops. It is a good wood for carving and is worked easily with tools. It takes a high polish like marble that shows its beautiful grain. Bookends, bowls, and trays of myrtle wood are common items in Oregon gift shops. Finished myrtle wood is the most expensive of western hardwoods. **In 1869, when the Union Pacific Railroads met in Utah, the golden spikes were pounded into a railroad tie made of polished myrtle wood.**

FILL IN THE BLANKS:

1. The Oregon myrtle is related to the

   _____ family.

2. When crushed, the leaves smell like

   _____.

3. _____ _____ is well known in gift shops.

4. a. _____ myrtle wood is the most expensive

   of western b. _____.

LOOK FOR THE WORD!

When you find a word, circle each letter in that word. When you find all
the words you will have some letters left. What is the secret word?

```
Ⓑ S N T S C E S S M M N L I K        BALK, BEAMS,
Ⓐ O E E H E E G A T O I S C A        BEECH, BOARD
Ⓛ A A E E K A H A I C A L G N        CELLULOSE
Ⓚ K R R A R O S T K P E N L D        CHERRY
T R L H D G G C O W N I F O S        CONSTRUCTION
Y O S C A O U R O N P I O E L        DEFECTS
C W T N E R O O E R E W R I D        EVERGREEN
L I Y U T L D W A V T D M H S        GOOD HEARTWOOD
A K N S N O L W D F E E Y T S        HEMLOCK
T C N A R L B U O E W D A L E        HOLE
H O L E G E A S L O R N A L P        HYDROGEN
C L H E A R T W O O D B P I G        KILN, LATH,
E M I M G O O D G A S A N K N        LIMEWOOD
E E S P R U C E R N M E G S I        MAHOGANY
B H R E S I N D O O W E S O R        MAPLE, MILLS
                                     ODOR, ORGANIC
                                     PINE
                                     REDWOOD
                                     RESIN, RING
                                     ROSEWOOD
                                     SAPWOOD
                                     SEASONED
                                     SHAKES
                                     SHRINKAGE
                                     SLABS, SKILL
                                     SOFTWOOD
                                     SPRUCE
                                     STANDARD
                                     TEAK, WALNUT
                                     WARPING, WORK
```

Letters left over: ___ ___ ___ ___ ___ ___ ___ ___

Look up the meaning of the word. It means:_____

_____

_____

The sun also rises, and the sun goes down, And hastens to the place where it arose. The wind goes toward the south, And turns around to the north; The wind whirls about continually, And comes again on its circuit (Ecclesiastes 1:5 & 6).

Oregon Weather

It has been said that Oregon has only one type of weather, and that's wet! Actually, there is no single "Oregon Climate." There are at least five Oregon climates.

Valley

This is the Willamette Valley. This area also has mild winters and summers. The end of the valley near Portland and the Columbia Gorge has weather that is a little colder because of the winter wind coming down the Columbia Gorge.

Mountains

This area is the Cascade Mountain Range, including Mount Hood and all the mountains south across the California border. This area has cold winters and pleasant summers.

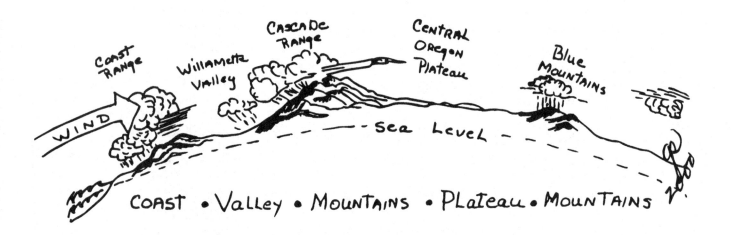

1. **Coastal**

2. **Valley**

3. **Mountain – Cascade Range**

4. **Plateau**

5. **Mountain – Blue, Wallowa**

Coastal

This is the area from the mouth of the Columbia River at Astoria to Brookings, near the California border. The coastal area has mild winters and mild summers. It is also one of the wettest parts of the state. This also includes the Coast Range.

Plateau

The plateau area is also known as the high desert, around the towns of Bend and Sisters, in central Oregon. This area has very cold winters and hot to mild summers. This area lies east of the Cascade Range and therefore does not get the rainfall that the coastal area receives. The rain is usually dropped on the mountains before reaching the high desert.

Eastern Mountains

This area includes the Blue Mountains and the Wallowa Mountains going south to the southeastern part of the state into the Steens Mountains. This area also has cold winters and mild summers.

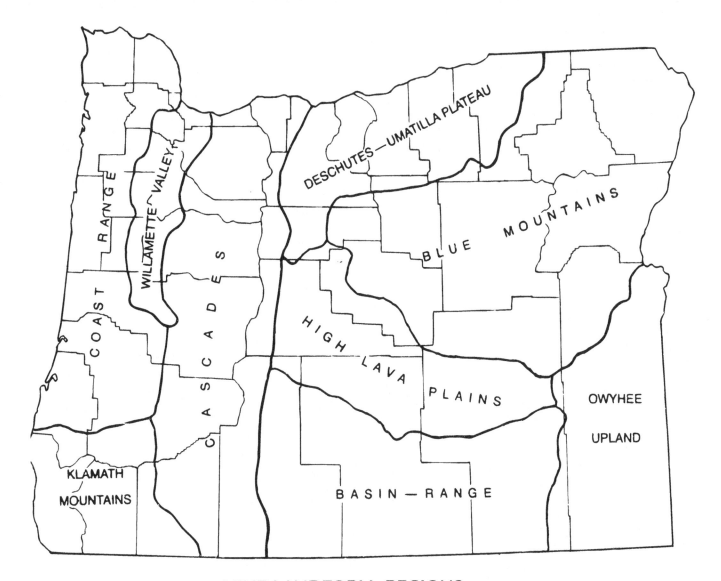

NINE LANDFORM REGIONS

1. Coast Range
2. Klamath Mountains
3. Willamette Vally
4. Cascades
5. Deschutes - Umatilla Plateau
6. High Lava Plains
7. Basin - Range
8. Blue Mountains
9. Owyhee Upland

*Color each region in the color of your choice.

I know that whatever God does, it shall be forever. Nothing can be added to it, and nothing taken from it. God does it, that men should fear before Him. That which is has already been, and what is to be has already been; And God requires an account of what is past (Ecclesiastes 3:14 & 15).

Discoveries In Oregon

Man has always been fascinated with the past. We have wondered what happened to the people back in the past. What did they eat? What did they wear? What did they talk about? How did they communicate?

In 1938, Dr. L.S. Cressman, an anthropologist from the University of Oregon, discovered a pair of sandals in a cave in Lake County. The sandals were exposed to a radiocarbon test. The test on the sandals found in the Fort Rock Cave indicated that man had lived in Oregon some 9,000 years ago.

At the Fort Rock Cave area, other traces of human life were found such as baskets, knives, arrowheads, and stones, which apparently were used to weigh down fishnets. No human skeletons were found.

There is another area in Oregon which has provided us with rich finds: **The John Day Fossil Beds in Grant County.** This area has attracted many miners of pre-historic lore. **Thomas Condon, a pioneer geologist,** first explored the area around John Day in **1865. Fossils of plant and animal life were found**.

Thomas Condon later discovered fossils around Fossil Lake in Lake County. This area is known as the Equua (horse) Beds of Oregon.

In the Fossil Lake area, evidence was found of several types of horses which once roamed the country, along with elephants, camels and other mammals. The discovery attracted fossil hunters from all over the United States.

In 1906 the Antiquities Act gave the president of the United States the power to protect places of special historic or scientific interest as national monuments. More than 100 national monuments have been designated in the past 90 years. Oregon has three: the Oregon Caves, the John Day Fossil Beds and Newberry National Volcanic Monument.

OREGON CAVES:

Designated in 1909 by President William Taft.

Defining feature: A natural marble cave. Above ground is an old growth forest. (480 acres)

Visitors: 90,000 in 1999.

JOHN DAY FOSSIL BEDS

Designated in 1974 by President Gerald Ford.

Defining feature: Fossils of plants and animals spanning more than 40 million of the 65 million years of the Cenozoic era (14,000 acres).

Visitors: 100,000 in 1999.

NEWBERRY NATIONAL VOLCANIC MONUMENT

Designated in 1990 by President George Bush.

Defining feature: The Big Obsidian Flow, created 1,300 years ago, covers 700 acres. The monument covers 55,500 acres.

Visitors: 60,000 in 1999.

There is so much to see in Oregon. Oregon has it all! From high mountains, ocean beaches, lava lands, fresh water fishing, water skiing on a river to mountain skiing on snow. Oregon has it all! Big caves, little caves, great big falls and little falls, Oregon has it all.

Be proud of our state. **It was created by God** and He meant that we should enjoy the beauty that He created.

FILL IN THE BLANKS:

1. In 1938, Dr. L.S. _____ , an anthropologist from the University of Oregon, discovered a pair of _____.

2. They were found in _____ _____ cave.

3. The sandals were exposed to a _____ - _____ test.

4. The test indicated that the sandals were about _____ years old.

5. Name two of the four things also found in the cave.

   a._____ , b. _____

6. Name another area in Oregon where you can find fossils _____.

7. Name the geologist who first explored the John Day area. _____.

8. The fossils were of a. _____ and

   b. _____ life.

USING YOUR DICTIONARY DEFINE THE FOLLOWING:

navigation _____

_____

_____

_____.

buoy _____

_____

_____.

dredge _____

_____

_____

_____.

export _____

_____

_____

_____.

grazing _____

_____

_____

_____.

All the rivers run into the sea, yet the sea is not full; to the place from which the rivers come, there they return again (Ecclesiastes 1:7).

Shipping

BRIG
Georgia Algar 2000

The mighty Columbia River is very important to the people of Oregon. The **Columbia River provides the inland city of Portland its only deep water shipping lane to the ocean**. Portland is unique among major Pacific Coast ports in that it is **110 miles inland**. River travel of 110 miles may not sound like much of a chore for a ship designed to survive the dangers of the open ocean. Rivers, particularly ones as long and mighty as the Columbia, have sneaky little tricks of their own. **The river has a bad habit of picking up tons of sand and depositing it in unlikely places**. A ship stuck on a sandbar might as well be tied up to a wharf.

The mouth of the Columbia has a very treacherous sandbar, which each ship must cross. Many a ship captain has studied a navigational chart showing an open channel in the Columbia River and steered a careful course only to have his ship run aground on a sandbar. That sandbar had not been there when his charts were printed.

Sand, billions of fine grains of it, are carried by the strong flowing river. Then underwater ridges are formed when the fresh river water meets the incoming tides of the ocean salt water from the ocean. Sometimes the sandpiles up in great soft heaps. These heaps can be so high that they jut above the surface of the water to form an island at low tide. This low island then hides beneath the surface

of the water when the tide flows in, and waits for the next victim to try to cross with his ship.

The area around the mouth of the Columbia River has been known as a "graveyard for ships." (Back in 1906 the ship *Peter Iredale* ran aground. That spot on Clatsop Beach is now a state park.)

There have been many victims of these wrecks. **Between 1850 and 1950, there were 150 major shipwrecks in the area around the mouth of the Columbia River.**

Jetties were constructed on both sides of the river to help control the sand buildup and keep a channel open. **Dredging** helped, also. **Navigational aids such as lighthouses and buoys were installed to mark a safe path**. World War II introduced the wide use of radar on ships. With each improvement, the mouth of the Columbia River has become a little less hazardous.

As traffic on the Columbia increased during the 1880s, it became clear that something would have to be done about the sand-clogged bars. If ships were to be able to take their goods up the river to Portland, the sand bars would have to be cleared out of the river. Some of the smaller ships from San Francisco had begun docking at St. Helens, 30 miles from Portland. They wanted to avoid the dangers of sand plugged waters at the mouth of the Willamette. **Any vessel drawing over 17 feet of water** (that is, sinking deeper than that into the water) did not stand much chance of reaching Portland and the dock.

In 1891, the Port of Portland was established to deal with these problems. First, dikes were built to

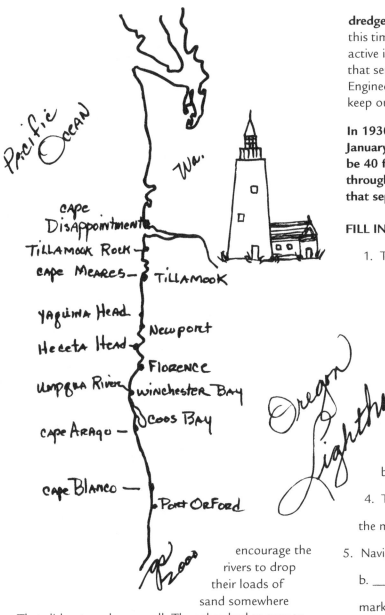

dredge and maintain a 30-foot channel. It was about this time that the federal government began to take an active interest in the development of the shipping channel that serves Portland. Since 1913, the U.S. Army Corps of Engineers has supplied money, equipment, and men to keep our waterways clear of the sand problem.

In 1930, a 35-foot channel project got underway. January 1964, work began on a channel that would now be 40 feet deep and 600 feet wide. This depth was to be throughout the entire 110 miles of sand-loaded river that separates Portland from the sea.

FILL IN THE BLANKS:

1. The a. _____ river gives inland

   Portland its only

   b. _____

   _____

   _____.

2. Portland is _____ miles inland.

3. Sand forms underwater ridges when the

   a. _____ water strikes the incoming

   b. _____water.

4. There have been _____ major shipwrecks around the mouth of the Columbia River.

5. Navigational aids such as a. _____ and

   b. _____ were installed to

   mark a safe path.

6. The first type of dredge was the a. _____ and

   b. _____ type.

7. In 1930 a _____ foot channel project got underway.

encourage the rivers to drop their loads of sand somewhere else. That did not work very well. Then they had to turn to dredging.

A *chain and bucket* dredge was tried. The chain and bucket dredge was nothing more than a mechanized shovel. Something stronger and faster was needed. It was provided in **1898 when the first hydraulic suction dredge went into operation. It was named the** *Portland*.

The *Portland* did a good job. It sucked the sand into a 20-inch pipe, then spewed it out through several hundred additional feet of pipe into a place where it wouldn't block the channel. Think of it as a huge floating vacuum cleaner. The *Portland* worked the rivers until 1922, when it collided with another ship and sank.

Now, 30-inch dredges were at work. Once a suction dredge went into operation, the days of a 17-foot deep channel were over. Work began **in 1913 on a plan to**

During World War I and World War II, shipbuilding was important to Oregon. **During World War I**, shipyards lined the river from Portland's central district to the St. Johns' district. **Most of the ships were built of wood from our own Oregon forests**.

When World War II renewed the United States' need for ships, the shipbuilding effort came again to Portland. **Ships in World War II were built of iron and steel**. Ships built in Oregon were very important to the winning of the war.

At **Tongue Point, near Astoria, the U.S. Navy has what they call their "mothball fleet."** These are ships that have their turrets coated with plastic and other measures to keep the salty air from eating away at the metal. These are ships that can be reactivated if needed.

Portland is our main shipping port, but Oregon also has some other ports. **One coastal port is at Newport.** At Newport, we have the second largest lumber and shipping port. **Another port is located at Coos Bay,** also a large lumber and shipping port.

Why is a shipping port so important? We have many things here in Oregon that we want to share with the rest of the United States and the people of the world.

One of the fastest ways to get these things to other people is to use a ship. We do have railroads, trucks, and air-planes, but ships can hold so much more cargo. Oregon ships out lumber cut in the Northwest. We also help to feed hungry people. **Two and one-half million tons of wheat was shipped from Portland in 1970. Lumber and wheat are just two of our large exports. In 1990 the export of wheat totaled 226,714 tons.**

On the other hand, we import from **Japan, China, and Brazil.** Japan has been one of Portland's best customers. We receive cars from Japan, including Toyota, Honda, and Isuzu autos.

Swan Island boasts one of the best dry-dock facilities on the Pacific Coast. This is where the large ships are repaired. **Dry Dock No. 3 at Swan Island is rated the third largest on the Pacific Coast.**

Yes! Shipping has been very important to Oregon.

FILL IN THE BLANKS:

1. During World War I, most ships were made of _____.

2. Ships built in World War II were made of a. _____ and b. _____.

3. What is at Tongue Point? _____.

4. Name two other Oregon Coastal ports besides Portland. a. _____ and b. _____.

5. Oregon ships out _____ cut in the Northwest.

6. Two and one-half million tons of _____ was shipped from Portland in 1970.

7. Name three countries we get imports from.
   a. _____, b. _____ and c. _____.

8. Swan Island boasts one of the best _____ facilities on the Pacific Coast.

9. Dry-dock # a. _____, at b. _____ _____is rated the c._____ largest on the Pacific Coast.

I made my works great, I built myself houses, and planted myself vineyards. I made myself gardens and orchards, and I planted all kinds of fruit trees in them (Ecclesiastes 2:4 & 5).

What WE Grow in Oregon

For crop farming, Oregon's Willamette Valley offers some very special conditions. **Oregon has become famous for its specialty crops**. Seed growing gets particular emphasis. No other place in the world grows more rye grass seed than Oregon. **Rye grass seed is a specialty crop**. Other production crops are snap beans, loganberries, blueberries, filberts, winter pears, sweet cherries, blackberries, red raspberries, boysenberries, youngberries, peppermint, strawberries, and several other seed crops. **Pumpkins, tomatoes, corn, potatoes, squash, cucumbers, and potatoes are some of the vegetables grown in Oregon.**

Oregon is known throughout the country for its **production of lily bulbs in Curry County**. Many other flower bulbs are grown for the open market.

Growing farm produce is no longer enough. We now are processing to preserve the product for shipment. **In Salem, Oregon, we find the second largest canning and freezing center in the United States**. Here great quantities of fruits, vegetables and berries are processed each year.

Hood River, Oregon, is famous for the production of apples, cherries, and pears. A large processing plant can be seen at Hood River.

Large fields of wheat, oats, barley and rye can be seen to the east, past The Dalles, along the Columbia River. Today wheat remains the most important commercial crop in Oregon. It is raised as a dry-land crop. The plateau areas of Oregon are very well suited for dry-land farming. Rainfall is sparse, from 10 to 20 inches per year, and it falls mainly during the winter months.

Generally, wheat is planted in alternate years. Thus the soil can accumulate one year's moisture before the next crop is planted.

Oats, barley, and corn for livestock feed are grown in the fields of the Northwest. Other feed crops include alfalfa, timothy, and clover.

Local markets take up the major part of these crops. Although horses no longer provide a large market for feed crops, as they once did, the raising of other livestock has maintained and even increased the demand.

FILL IN THE BLANKS:

1. Oregon has become famous for its

   _____ crops.

2. _____ seed is a specialty

   crop.

3. Oregon is known for its production of

   a. _____ bulbs in

   b. _____ County.

4. The second largest a. _____ and

   b. _____ center is located in Salem.

5. Large fields of _____ can be seen past The Dalles.

6. Name three livestock feed crops. a. _____ b.

   _____ and c. _____.

Some Animals In Oregon

BEEF CATTLE

Today **beef cattle and dairy cattle** form the basis for two separate large industries in Oregon. The production of beef cattle can be divided into **two categories: cattle raised on range lands and cattle raised on farms**.

Few of the big cattle ranches common from about 1860 to 1890 exist today. The great cattle drives belong to the past. The open ranges are now, for the most part, fenced in.

Oregon produces about 500,000 head of beef cattle annually. Today's herds are largely made up of Herefords, polled Herefords, Aberdeen Angus and short-horns.

DAIRY CATTLE

The dairy industry is highly mechanized. **Dairymen must invest large sums of money in equipment and good grazing land.** Good grazing land and a supply of supplemental grain and forage are necessary to keep the cows producing milk. Since milk constitutes the major dairy products, **dairies need to be located near centers of population.**

Some of the dairy cows we have in Oregon are Jersey, Holstein and Guernsey.

FILL IN THE BLANKS:

1. What are the two main cattle industries in Oregon? a. _____ and b. _____.

2. Name two of the four beef cattle found in Oregon. a. _____ and b. _____.

3. Dairymen must invest in a. _____ and good b. _____ land.

4. Dairy farms need to be located near centers of _____.

5. Name the three types of dairy cows in Oregon. a. _____ b. _____ and c. _____.

SHEEP

Today flocks of sheep still move from the lowlands to the mountains with the seasons. Now, however, when the sheep are ready for the market, they go by train or truck instead of moving by foot along the overland trails.

Oregon ranks second in sheep production. Idaho leads, with Washington State in third place. **Sheep are raised not only for their meat but also their fine grade of wool.** The wool is used to make such articles of clothing as sweaters, hats, gloves, mittens, suits, jackets and many other items.

POULTRY

The poultry industry is also very highly specialized. **Some poultrymen concentrate on raising flocks for egg production, while others raise chickens primarily for the meat.** Some may specialize in the production of "fryers" while some raise only "broilers." Poultrymen also specialize in the hatching of baby chicks for sale to egg producers and meat producers.

The development of **better storage facilities for eggs and new methods of freezing meat have broadened the market for poultry products.** Today both eggs and meat from the Northwest are sold in eastern markets. **Approximately one billion eggs are produced in Washington and about two-thirds that number are produced in Oregon**.

Turkey production is increasing in importance, thanks to the development of small birds. Over a million turkeys are now sold annually. They are raised on both sides of the Cascades, though the dry climate east of the mountains is more favorable for the production of poults, or young turkeys.

FILL IN THE BLANKS:

1. Oregon ranks _____ in sheep production.

2. Sheep are raised not only for their

   a. _____ but also for their fine grade of

   b. _____.

3. Some poultrymen concentrate on raising flocks of

   chickens for _____ production.

4. Better storage facilities for eggs and new methods of

   _____ meat have broadened the market.

Food we grow in Oregon

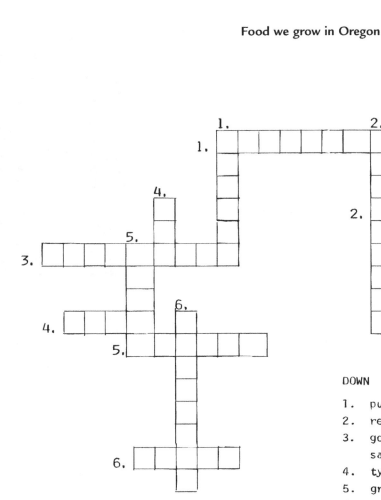
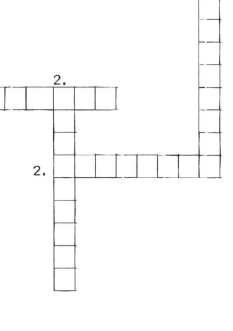

ACROSS

1. dark berry
2. large orange globes
3. best in muffins
4. pops easily
5. mash down
6. makes bread

DOWN

1. put in horse feed
2. red berry
3. goes with bacon and lettuce sandwich
4. type of bread
5. green, string, lima and such
6. makes pickles

113

UNIT VI

MULTIPLE CHOICE

1. The great fire of 1933 was started by: a. matches   b. a campfire   c. friction

2. The fire was named: a. The Great Fire   b. The Tillamook Burn   c. The Oregon Fire

3. The smoke could be seen all the way to: a. Newport   b. Bend   c. Portland

4. The fire was caused by man's: a. concern   b. carelessness   c. thinking

5. The Douglas fir was named after: a. General Douglas MacArthur   b. David Douglas   c. Douglas Fairbanks

6. The company that built the *vee-balloons* was: a. NASA   b. McDonald-Douglas   c. Goodyear Aerospace

MATCHING

7. _____	Name the two kinds of trees.	A. Myrtle wood
8. _____	Conifer comes from this word.	B. Aircraft
9. _____	In WWI the Sitka spruce was used for making.	C. Dr. L.S. Cressman
10. _____	Sitka spruce can grow as tall as.	D. mistletoe
11. _____	The resin inside the juniper berry emits a.	E. Needleleaf and Broadleaf
12. _____	Grows in the tops or crowns of the white oak.	F. Swan Island
13. _____	Leaves of the Oregon Myrtle smell like.	G. 9000 years
14. _____	Is a part of the Laurel family.	H. 180 feet
15. _____	Was found at Fort Rock Cave.	I. Cone
16. _____	The sandals were about how old.	J. John Day Fossil Beds
17. _____	We can find a lot of fossils here.	K. pungent smell
18. _____	The man who found the sandals.	L. Portland
19. _____	Is 110 miles inland.	M. camphor
20. _____	Dry-dock #3 is where?	N. sandals

TRUE OR FALSE

21. _____ East, past The Dalles, we grow tomatoes and cucumbers.

22. _____ We freeze only vegetables at the plant in Salem.

23. _____ We have three types of dairy cows in Oregon, Jersey, Holstein and Guernsey.

24. _____ Oregon ranks second in sheep production.

25. _____ Better storage for eggs and new freezing methods for meats have broadened the market.

114

NOW GO BACK AND STUDY ALL THE QUESTIONS FOR UNIT VI TO PREPARE FOR THE FINAL TEST.

Suggested Projects

1. Do a special report on the big fire of 1988 in Yellowstone National Park.

2. If you can, visit a lumber mill with your parents. See how the logs are cut into boards.

3. Be a "reporter" for a day and interview a "logger."

4. Read the weather report in the newspaper every day for two weeks, and track the weather pattern in your area.

5. Plant something, a small garden crop of vegetables or maybe some strawberry plants. Care for them, water them, and when you harvest them, eat and enjoy them. Don't forget to share the harvest with your family!

6. Get information on the airplane named the "Spruce Goose." Who built it? Where can you see it now? Do a 250-word report.

Oregon History

S T U D E N T   W O R K B O O K

UNIT VII
Oregon Facts

- Mountains
- Symbols
- Landmarks

STUDENTS' GOAL	
Target Test Date	_____
Pages in Unit	_____
Pages Per Day	_____
Date Unit Completed	_____
Final Score of Unit	_____

UNIT VII
Oregon Facts

The word *Oregon* has numerous supposed origins, each of them beautiful. Some of them are:

OYER-UN-GEN, a Shoshone Indian word for "place of plenty."

AURA AGUA, a Spanish word meaning, "gently falling waters."

WAU-RE-GAN, an Algonquin word meaning, "beautiful water."

No matter how you pronounce the name of our beautiful state, it is still a very special place to live.

Some authorities think that Oregon's name came from the name that the Columbia River was once called, the Oregon or **Ouragan**, which means "hurricane" in French. Another thought is that the name

Oregon is Spanish meaning, "wild thyme." Whatever its origins, we are blessed to be living in such a wonderful and beautiful place.

Our state of Oregon has so much to offer. Anything you may want to experience can be found in our state. From snow skiing to water skiing, from mountain climbing to desert walking, from fossil hunting to lava rock walking, from white-water rapid boating to crashing Pacific Coast waves to leisurely fly fishing, you will find it all in our great state of Oregon.

As early as 1765, a Massachusetts man, Major Robert Rogers (who served in the British campaigns against the French), petitioned the British government to support an expedition from the Great Lakes toward the headwaters of the Mississippi River. They then wanted to push on to the river the Indians called *Ouragon*. He never made the trip, but the word Oregon was down on paper and in history.

To read more about Major Robert Rogers, go to your local library and get a book titled, **Northwest Passage** by the author, Kenneth Roberts, Doubleday, Doran & Co., Inc., 1937. This is a fictional book based on fact. It is known as an historical novel.

STATE SONG

OREGON, MY OREGON

Land of the Empire Builders,
Land of the Golden West;
Conquered and held by freeman,
Fairest and the best.
Onward and Upward ever;
Forward and on and on
Hail to thee, Land of Heroes, My Oregon.

Land of the rose and sunshine,
Land of the summer's breeze;
Laden with health and vigor,
Fresh from the Western seas.
Blest by the blood of martyrs,
Land of the setting sun;
Hail to thee, Land of Promise, My Oregon.

(Oregon State Song, words by J.A. Buchanan)*

*Music may be found in the Oregon Blue Book, 1967-68, pp. 133. Copies available from the Secretary of State, Salem, Oregon.

FACTS AT A GLANCE
OREGON

State Capital ....Salem

Total Area ....96,981 square miles
(10th largest state in
the United States)

Population

12,093 (1850 census)	1,521,341 (1950 census)
52,465 (1860 census)	1,768,687 (1960 census)
174,768 (1880 census)	2,633,149 (1980 census)
317,704 (1890 census)	2,842,321 (1990 census)
	3,421,399 (2000 census)

Elevation.......................................Sea level to 11, 240
feet (Mount Hood)

Major Industries ....Lumber, agriculture,
beef and dairy cattle.

First Provisional Government 1843

Territorial Status 1848

Statehood.....................................1859

State Motto (1987).......................*Alis Volat Propiis*
(She Flies With Her
Own Wings)

Old State Motto (1957) ...."The Union"

State Colors ....Navy blue and gold

State Tree ....Douglas fir

State Fish ....Chinook salmon

State Rock ....Thunderegg

State Animal ....Beaver

State Bird ....Western meadowlark

State Flower ....Oregon grape

State Beverage.............................Milk

State Gemstone...........................Oregon sunstone

State Insect ....Oregon swallowtail

State Dance ....Square dance

State Nut ....Hazelnut (filbert)

State Seashell ....Oregon hairy triton

Counties 36

OREGON STATE SEAL

The state seal was adopted in 1859.

In September 1857, a resolution was adopted by the Constitutional Convention to authorize the president to appoint a committee to report on a proper device for the seal of the state of Oregon.

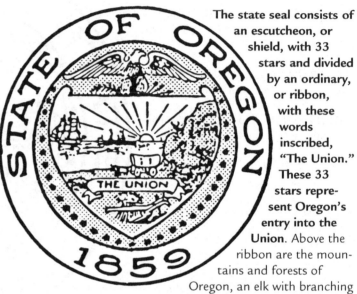

The state seal consists of an escutcheon, or shield, with 33 stars and divided by an ordinary, or ribbon, with these words inscribed, "The Union." These 33 stars represent Oregon's entry into the Union. Above the ribbon are the mountains and forests of Oregon, an elk with branching antlers, a covered wagon and ox team, the Pacific Ocean with setting sun. The covered wagon and oxen depict the pioneers that came to the state in the 1840s and 1850s. The departing British man-of-war and arriving American merchant ship symbolize the end of British influence and the rise of American power. The sheaf of grain, the pickax, and the plow represent Oregon's mining and agricultural resources. The crest is the American eagle. Around the perimeter of the seal is the legend "State of Oregon, 1859."

The old state motto, *The Union* is the motto that was adopted in 1957.

The new state motto, *Alis Volat Propiis*, translates from the Latin as "She Flies With Her Own Wings." This new motto was adopted by the 1987 legislature to replace the old motto.

COUNTIES LISTED ALPHABETICALLY

BAKER	CROOK	HARNEY	LAKE	MORROW	UNION
BENTON	CURRY	HOOD RIVER	LANE	MULTNOMAH	WALLOWA
CLACKAMAS	DESCHUTES	JACKSON	LINCOLN	POLK	WASCO
CLATSOP	DOUGLAS	JEFFERSON	LINN	SHERMAN	WASHINGTON
COLUMBIA	GILLIAM	JOSEPHINE	MALHEUR	TILLAMOOK	WHEELER
COOS	GRANT	KLAMATH	MARION	UMATILLA	YAMHILL

OREGON STATE FLAG

Oregon was the 33rd state to join the Union of the United States. On its flag, proudly displayed are 33 gold stars on a navy blue background. **The official flag, adopted in 1925**, also bears the escutcheon, which forms the major part of the state seal. The letters that spell out "State of Oregon," and the date 1859, are also gold in color.

The flag is a replica of the state seal without the circular border. On the reverse side of the flag is a beaver in gold, significant of the nickname for our state, "**The Beaver State**."

STATE NICKNAME —THE BEAVER STATE

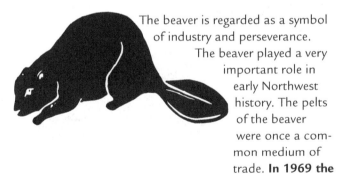

The beaver is regarded as a symbol of industry and perseverance. The beaver played a very important role in early Northwest history. The pelts of the beaver were once a common medium of trade. **In 1969 the beaver was made the official state animal.**

STATE COLORS —NAVY BLUE AND GOLD

STATE TREE —DOUGLAS FIR

The first white men to observe the Douglas fir were probably Lewis and Clark. The man to give a name to our state tree was a Scottish botanist, named David Douglas. It is named in honor of David Douglas. The Douglas fir is a member of the pine family but not a true fir.

This tree has great strength, stiffness and moderate weight that make it an invaluable timber product. It is said to be stronger than concrete. It averages up to 200 feet in height and 6 feet in diameter. It has even been found at heights of up to 325 feet and in diameters of up to 15 feet.

The foliage on a mature tree is most often a deep yellow-green and its 2-inch to 4-inch cones fall intact. The Douglas fir is found mostly in the region **west of the Cascade Mountain range.** It outranks any other individual North American pine in lumber uses and lumber products.

The Douglas fir was adopted as the official state tree in 1939.

STATE FISH —CHINOOK SALMON

The Chinook salmon, is a member of the Salmonidae fish family, which includes salmons proper, trout, and chars. The Chinook salmon is also known as spring, king and tyee salmon. The Chinook salmon is the largest of the Pacific salmon. Its average length is 36 inches to 58 inches. The Chinook is a prized sport fish. It is found in larger rivers from California to as far north as Alaska. Record catches have been reported as 53 inches, weighing 126 pounds.

The Chinook salmon was designated as the official state fish in 1961 by the Oregon legislature.

STATE BIRD
—WESTERN MEADOWLARK

The Western meadowlark is part of the family of birds that includes blackbirds and orioles. Its average size is from 9 inches to 11 inches long. The bird is native to all parts of the state. It ranges from southern and southwest Canada through central and western United States to the highlands of central Mexico.

This bird has a brownish-cream breast streaked with bright yellow, crossed by a black V. Our Western meadowlark is distinguished from its eastern cousin by a more melodic song and lighter brown streaking on its head.

The Western meadowlark lives in grasslands, cultivated fields and pastures, meadows, and prairies. It builds a domed shaped nest on the ground.

The beautiful and distinctive song of the Western meadowlark sets it apart from other birds.

In 1927 Oregon schoolchildren participated in a poll sponsored by the Oregon Audubon Society. In this poll the children chose the Western meadowlark as the state bird.

The bird enjoys a diet of plant seeds and grains in the winter. In the summer it eats large insects, spiders, snails, some other birds' eggs, and carrion. It is known as omnivorous.

The Western meadowlark became the official state bird in 1927.

STATE FLOWER
—OREGON GRAPE

The Oregon grape, a wild plant, is also called the Oregon holly-grape. The Oregon grape is neither a grape nor a holly. It belongs to the barberry family.

The Oregon grape grows from western Oregon through western Washington and northward into British Columbia. The Oregon grape is a plant grown close to the ground. It does not climb like a wild grape does. Its leaves look like those of the holly and its wood is yellow. The clusters of dainty yellow flowers open in early summer. The berries ripen late in the fall, and look like grapes or blueberries. The berries of this plant are often used to make jelly.

The Oregon grape became the official state flower in 1899.

STATE ROCK
—THUNDEREGG

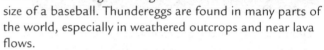

Thundereggs are sometimes referred to as a geode, a nodule, or a "rhodolite bomb." They vary in size from that of a small marble, to a large boulder four to five feet across. The average size might be the size of a baseball. Thundereggs are found in many parts of the world, especially in weathered outcrops and near lava flows.

The thunderegg is generally round in shape. The contents, which vary from one location to another, have included agates, quartz, opal, gilsonite (a residue of oil), and even uranium in small quantities.

When it is sliced open, the thunderegg might reveal a star-shaped pattern with brightly colored parallel bands. The thunderegg is found chiefly in the Oregon counties of Crook, Jefferson, Malheur, Wasco, and Wheeler.

The thunderegg became the official state rock in 1965 after rockhounds throughout Oregon voted it their first choice.

STATE ANIMAL
—BEAVER

The beaver has soft brown fur, a flat broad tail, chisel-like teeth, and can live on land as well as in the water. Its body is thickset and can grow to be three feet long and weigh up to 60 pounds or more. Its tail is not only flat, but also scaly, measuring about a foot long. The tail serves as a handy rudder in the water, and a danger signal for other beaver when slapped on the ground.

The beaver has been referred to as "nature's engineer," and its dam-building activities are important to natural water flow and erosion control.

In the early days, before Oregon became a state, the Indians, fur trappers, and mountain men trapped the beaver for its soft fur. They traded the fur pelts for supplies.

In 1969 the beaver became the official state animal. The Oregon State University's athletic teams are called the "Beavers."

STATE INSECT —OREGON SWALLOWTAIL

The Oregon legislature in 1979 designated the Oregon swallowtail to be Oregon's state insect. This butterfly is a true native of the Northwest. The Oregon swallowtail is at home in the lower parts of sagebrush in the canyons of the Columbia River and its tributaries. This also includes the Snake River area. This beautiful butterfly is predominantly yellow, is wary of predators, and is a strong flier who is not easily captured.

STATE GEMSTONE —OREGON SUNSTONE

The Oregon sunstone was designated as the official state gemstone by the 1987 legislature. Uncommon in its composition, clarity, and colors, this stone is a large, brightly colored transparent gem in the feldspar family. The Oregon sunstone attracts collectors and miners and has been identified as a boon to tourism and economic development in southeastern Oregon counties.

STATE BEVERAGE —MILK

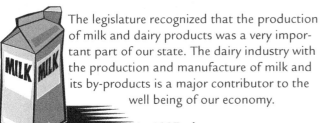

The legislature recognized that the production of milk and dairy products was a very important part of our state. The dairy industry with the production and manufacture of milk and its by-products is a major contributor to the well being of our economy.

In 1997, the legislature selected milk as the state beverage.

STATE DANCE —SQUARE DANCE

The square dance became the state dance when declared by the legislature in 1977. This dance combines a

variety of steps and figures danced with four couples grouped in a square. The pioneer spirit is reflected in the steps of the dance and the characteristic dress. It is an example of the heritage and friendly, enthusiastic free-spirited nature of our pioneer ancestors.

FATHER OF OREGON —DR. JOHN McCLOUGHLIN

In 1957 the legislature named Dr. John McLoughlin to receive the honorary title "Father of Oregon." This was in recognition of all of his contributions to the early development of the Oregon country. Dr. McLoughlin was instrumental in helping the missionaries Jason Lee and Dr. Marcus Whitman settle in the area to minister to the Indians. Without his help the missionaries and some of the mountain men would never have made it through the first winter.

Dr. McLoughlin came to the Northwest region in 1824 as the Chief Factor for the Hudson's Bay Company.

MOTHER OF OREGON —TABITHA BROWN

In 1987 the state legislature honored Tabitha Moffatt Brown as the "Mother of Oregon." She was chosen because her life represented the distinctive pioneer heritage, charitable and compassionate nature of Oregon's people. She was 66 years of age when she came to Oregon on a wagon train accompanied by her brother-in-law, who was 77 years old. She arrived with only a picayune, worth about six cents, in her glove. She multiplied this small amount into a school for children, and eventually founded Tualatin Academy, which is now Pacific University located in Forest Grove.

CRATER LAKE

CRATER LAKE is the deepest lake in the entire United States. It is 1,932 feet deep.

Major Mountains

CASCADE MOUNTAIN RANGE

The highest in elevation is Mount Hood at 11,240 feet. Mount Jefferson, Mount Washington, and Three Sisters all run from north to south in the state of Oregon. These mountains, which lie about 100 to 150 miles inland from the Pacific Coast, form an important climatic divide. They receive an abundant amount of rain on their western slopes but very little on the eastern slopes. The western slopes are heavily wooded, while the eastern slopes, are covered mainly by grasses and scrub plants. Many lakes and several large rivers are in the mountains. These mountains are used for outdoor recreation, including camping, hiking and snow and water skiing.

COAST RANGE

The Coast Range runs the length of the state of Oregon along the western coastline, from the Columbia River in the north to the Rogue River in the south. The highest in elevation is Mount Bolivar with 4,319 feet, followed by Mary's Peak at 4,097 feet. These mountains contain dense softwood forests, which historically made lumbering an important economic activity. The eastern slopes of the Coast Range mark the western edge of the Willamette Valley.

BLUE MOUNTAINS

This northeastern Oregon mountain chain is part of the Columbia Plateau, which extends into southeastern Washington. Lava flows cover much of the surface, and the upper, wooded slopes have been used for lumbering, recreation and livestock grazing, are the principle economic uses. The highest elevation is Rock Creek Butte at 9,105 feet, located on the Elkhorn Ridge, a few miles west of Baker City.

STEENS MOUNTAIN

This is a massive, 30-mile long mountain in the Alvord Valley. It features valleys and U-shaped gorges that were cut by glaciers over time. It is located in Harney County in southeastern Oregon, and is 9,773 feet in elevation.

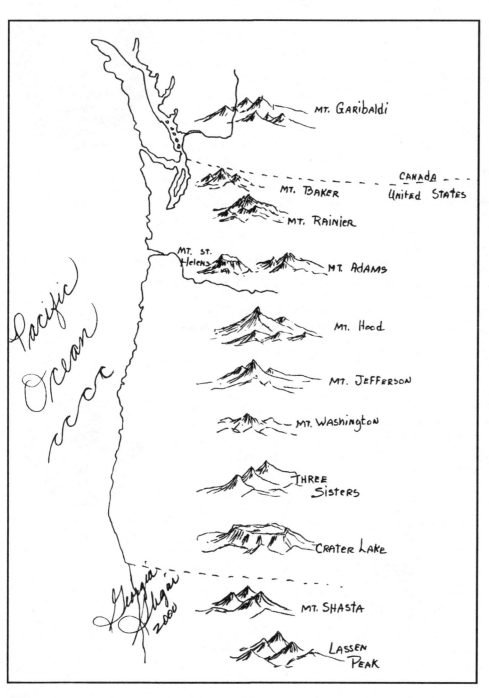

MAJOR DAMS

Bonneville Dam   –   Columbia River - 1938
The Dalles Dam   –   Columbia River - 1957
John Day Dam   –   Columbia River - 1968
McNary Dam   –   Columbia River - 1954
Owyhee Dam   –   Owyhee River   - 1932

MAJOR LIGHTHOUSES

Cape Meares   1890
Yaquina Head   1873
Yaquina Bay   1871
Heceta Head   1894
Umpqua River   1894
Cape Arago   1934
Coquille River   1896
Cape Blanco   1870

Using your dictionary, define the following:

1. **escutcheon** _____

_____

_____

_____

2. **diameter** _____

_____

_____

_____

3. **omnivorous** _____

_____

_____

_____

4. **geode** _____

_____

_____

_____

5. **transparent** _____

_____

_____

_____

MATCHING

1. _____	The state song	A. Chinook salmon
2. _____	The state capital	B. Hazelnut
3. _____	Elevation of Mount Hood	C. 1859
4. _____	Date of first provisional government	D. Cascade Range
5. _____	Date of territorial status	E. 11,240 feet
6. _____	Date of statehood	F. Navy blue & gold
7. _____	Old state motto	G. Oregon grape
8. _____	New state motto	H. Oregon swallowtail
9. _____	State colors	I. Oregon, My Oregon
10. _____	State tree	J. Beaver
11. _____	State fish	K. 1848
12. _____	State rock	L. 36
13. _____	State animal	M. "She Flies With Her Own Wings"
14. _____	State bird	N. Oregon sunstone
15. _____	State flower	O. Milk
16. _____	State beverage	P. Salem
17. _____	State gemstone	Q. Thunderegg
18. _____	State insect	R. 1843
19. _____	State dance	S. Oregon hairy triton
20. _____	State nut	T. Douglas fir
21. _____	State seashell	U. "The Union"
22. _____	Number of counties	V. Crater Lake
23. _____	Major mountain range	W. Western meadowlark
24. _____	Major lake	X. Bonneville, McNary, Owyhee, John Day, The Dalles
25. _____	Major dams	Y. Square dance

NOW GO BACK AND STUDY ALL THE QUESTIONS FOR UNIT VII TO PREPARE FOR THE FINAL TEST.

Suggested Projects

1. Look in magazines and newspapers to find pictures of all that we have studied in this Unit. Make your own picture notebook.

2. Choose four of your favorite subjects in this Unit and do a 250-word report on the four. A trip to your library might be helpful.

3. Take a trip to a local travel bureau or agency and explain that you are doing an Oregon history report and see how many tourist pamphlets you can obtain.

4. Have your Mom and Dad help you build a large to medium size shadow picture frame. Now select some seashells, wild flowers, or neat and colorful rocks or geodes to put in the frame as a display. Hang it on your bedroom wall.

5. Using our own state seal as an example, draw your own seal. Look up some of your ancestors. Did they come by wagon or boat? Draw a family shield or crest and put it all in color. Add your family name to a ribbon or banner below or above the seal.

Oregon History

STUDENT WORKBOOK

UNIT VIII

Oregon Counties

- Maps
- Information
- Places to Visit

STUDENTS' GOAL	
Target Test Date	_____
Pages in Unit	_____
Pages Per Day	_____
Date Unit Completed	_____
Final Score of Unit	_____

UNIT VIII
Oregon Counties

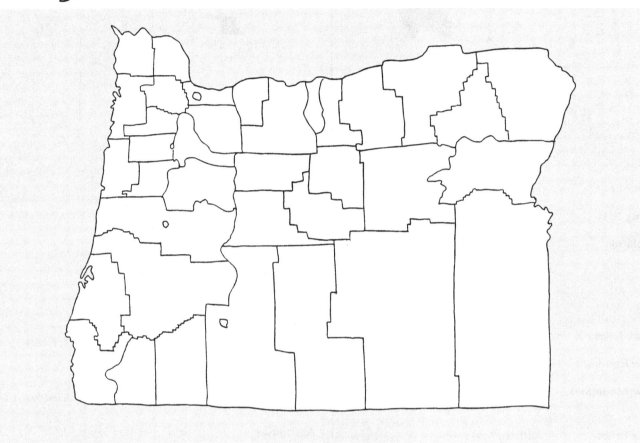

COUNTIES
AND COUNTY SEATS

1.	Baker	Baker City	19.	Lake	Lakeview
2.	Benton	Corvallis	20.	Lane	Eugene
3.	Clackamas	Oregon City	21.	Lincoln	Newport
4.	Clatsop	Astoria	22.	Linn	Albany
5.	Columbia	St. Helens	23.	Malheur	Vale
6.	Coos	Coquille	24.	Marion	Salem
7.	Crook	Prineville	25.	Morrow	Heppner
8.	Curry	Gold Beach	26.	Multnomah	Portland
9.	Deschutes	Bend	27.	Polk	Dallas
10.	Douglas	Roseberg	28.	Sherman	Moro
11.	Gilliam	Condon	29.	Tillamook	Tillamook
12.	Grant	Canyon City	30.	Umatilla	Pendleton
13.	Harney	Burns	31.	Union	La Grande
14.	Hood River	Hood River	32.	Wallowa	Enterprise
15.	Jackson	Medford	33.	Wasco	The Dalles
16.	Jefferson	Madras	34.	Washington	Hillsboro
17.	Josephine	Grants Pass	35.	Wheeler	Fossil
18.	Klamath	Klamath Falls	36.	Yamhill	Mc Minnville

BAKER COUNTY

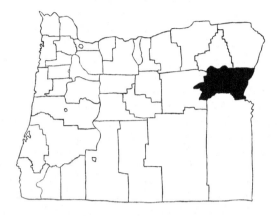

Established	September 22, 1862
County Seat	Baker City
Population	1970 – 14,919
	1976 – 15,950
	1980 – 16,134
	1990 – 15,317
	2000 – 16,741
Square Miles	3,068
Major Rivers	Snake River, Powder River
Major Mountains	Wallowa-Whitman National Forest, Whitman National Forest
Major Lakes	Anthony Lakes
Industry	lumber, machinery, and transportation equipment
Agriculture	dairy products, hay, and wheat
Logging	ponderosa pine
Livestock	dairy cattle

Places to Visit

- Anthony Lakes
- Old Oregon Trail
- Gold dredge in Sumpter
- Hells Canyon
- Ghost town near Sumpter and Bourne
- Oregon Trail Interpretive Center near Baker
- Sumpter Valley Dredge State Park
- Unity Lake State Park
- Wallowa-Whitman National Forest

BENTON COUNTY

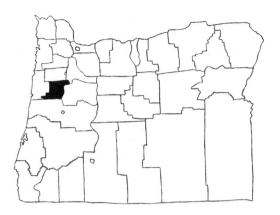

Established	December 23, 1847
County Seat	Corvallis
Population	1970 – 53,776
	1976 – 65,600
	1980 – 68,211
	1990 – 70,811
	2000 – 78,153
Square Miles	676
Major Rivers	Willamette River
Major Mountains	Siuslaw National Forest, Coast Range
Major Lakes	none
Industry	plywood, machinery, canneries
Agriculture	field seed, hay, vegetables
Logging	Douglas fir and hemlock
Livestock	dairy cattle

Places to Visit

- Oregon State University in Corvallis
- Horner Museum on Oregon State University Campus
- Mary's Peak
- William L. Finley National Wildlife Refuge
- Teacher's College in Philomath
- Old Benton County Courthouse and Clock Tower
- Corvallis Art Center
- Avery Park
- Gill Coliseum

CLACKAMAS COUNTY

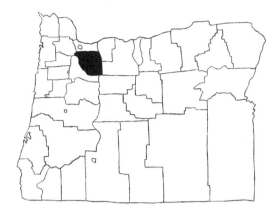

Established	July 5, 1843
County Seat	Oregon City
Population	1970 – 166,088
	1976 – 204,800
	1980 – 241,911
	1990 – 278,850
	2000 – 338,391
Square Miles	1,868
Major Rivers	Willamette River, Clackamas River, Snake River, Molalla River
Major Mountains	Mount Hood National Forest, Table Rock Wilderness
Major Lakes	none
Industry	paper, machinery, transportation equipment
Agriculture	fruits, nuts and berries
Logging	Douglas fir, hemlock, western red cedar
Livestock	dairy cattle

Places to Visit

- Oregon City (first capital)
- McLoughlin House in Oregon City
- Willamette Falls in Oregon City
- Mount Hood and Timberline Lodge
- Wilhoit Mineral Springs
- Old Barlow Road
- Bull of the Woods Wilderness
- End of the Oregon Trail Interpretive Center near Oregon City
- Bonnie Lake State Park

CLATSOP COUNTY

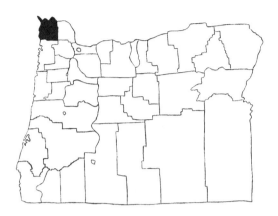

Established	June 22, 1844
County Seat	Astoria
Population	1970 – 28,473
	1976 – 29,500
	1980 – 32,489
	1990 – 33,301
	2000 – 35,630
Square Miles	827
Major Rivers	Columbia River, Young's River, Lewis and Clark River
Major Mountains	Clatsop State Forest
Major Lakes	none
Industry	lumber, plywood, paper, shipping, commercial fish canneries
Agriculture	wheat
Exports	logs and wheat
Logging	Douglas fir, hemlock, western red cedar

Places to Visit

- Fort Clatsop National Memorial
- Astoria Column
- Flavel Mansion Museum
- Columbia River Maritime Museum
- Fort Stevens State Park
- Tillamook Head
- Arch Cape
- Saddle Mountain State Park
- Young's River Falls County Park
- South Jetty
- Clatsop Spit

COLUMBIA COUNTY

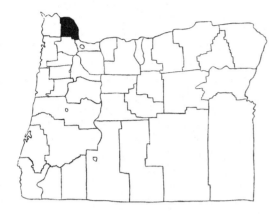

Established	January 16, 1854
County Seat	St. Helens
Population	1970 – 28,790
	1976 – 32,400
	1980 – 35,646
	1990 – 37,557
	2000 – 43,560
Square Miles	656
Major Rivers	Columbia River, Nehalem River, Clatskanie River
Major Mountains	Coast Range, Clatskanie Mountain
Major Lakes	none
Industry	paper, plywood, lumber
Agriculture	fruits, hay
Livestock	dairy cows
Logging	Douglas fir, hemlock, western red cedar

Places to Visit

- Rainier Nuclear Plant (closed)
- Lower Sauvie Island
- Longview Bridge
- Paper mill in St. Helens
- Banks-Vernonia State Park
- Bunker Hill

COOS COUNTY

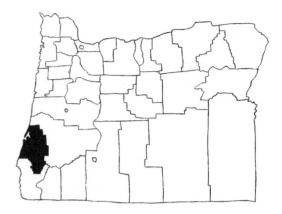

Established	December 22, 1853
County Seat	Coquille
Population	1970 – 56,515
	1976 – 60,200
	1980 – 64,047
	1990 – 60,273
	2000 – 62,779
Square Miles	1,600
Major Rivers	Coquille River, South Fork Coos River
Major Mountains	Elliott State Forest, north end Siskiyou National Forest
Major Lakes	Ten-mile Lake
Industry	plywood, lumber, boxes, paper
Agriculture	cattle, hay
Logging	Douglas fir, hemlock, western red cedar

Places to Visit

- Cape Arago
- Coos Bay South Slough
- Coquille Myrtle Grove State Park
- Fishing fleet at Coos Bay
- Coos Bay shipping port
- Cranberry bogs of Bandon
- Coquille River Estuary
- Hoffman Memorial Wayside

CROOK COUNTY

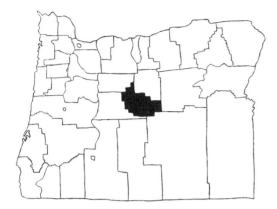

Established   October 24, 1882

County Seat   Prineville

Population
1970 – 9,985
1976 – 11,950
1980 – 13,091
1990 – 14,111
2000 – 19,182

Square Miles   2,979

Major Rivers   Crooked River

Major Mountains Ochoco National Forest, Maury Mountains

Major Lakes   Ochoco Lake

Industry   plywood and lumber

Agriculture   hay, potatoes

Livestock   cattle

Logging   ponderosa pine

Places to Visit

- Crooked River Canyon and Gorge
- Prineville Reservoir State Park
- Mill Creek Wilderness
- Smith Rock State Park
- Steins Pillar
- Central Oregon Timber Carnival
- Lava formations
- Rockhound areas
- Crooked River Roundup

CURRY COUNTY

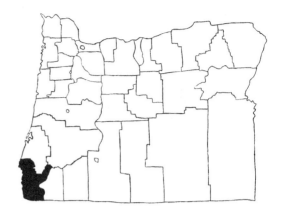

Established   December 18, 1855

County Seat   Gold Beach

Population
1970 – 13,006
1976 – 14,300
1980 – 16,992
1990 – 19,327
2000 – 21,137

Square Miles   1,627

Major Rivers   Rogue River, Elk River, Chetco River, Pistol River

Major Mountains Siskiyou National Forest

Major Lakes   Garrison Lake

Industry   plywood and lumber

Agriculture   nursery plants, cranberries

Livestock   cattle, dairy cows

Logging   Douglas fir, hemlock

Places to Visit

- Cape Blanco Lighthouse north of Port Orford
- Elk River Fish Hatchery
- Rogue River north of Gold Beach
- Battle Rock in Port Orford
- Myrtle groves
- Rogue River Trail
- Prehistoric gardens
- Cape Sebastian
- Paradise Point
- Loeb State Park
- Humbug Mountain

DESCHUTES COUNTY

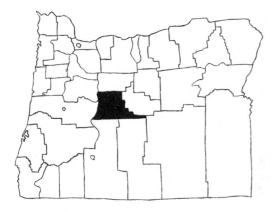

Established	December 13, 1916
County Seat	Bend
Population	1970 – 30,422
	1976 – 41,800
	1980 – 62,142
	1990 – 74,958
	2000 – 115,367
Square Miles	3,018
Major Rivers	Deschutes River, Metolius River
Major Mountains	Bachelor Butte, Mount Washington, Deschutes National Forest
Major Lakes	Paulina Lake, East Lake, Elk Lake, Lava Lake
Industry	plywood, lumber, textiles
Agriculture	hay, potatoes, wheat
Livestock	cattle, poultry, dairy products
Logging	ponderosa, lodgepole pine

Places to Visit

- Century Drive
- Paulina Lake
- Newberry Crater at Newberry National Volcanic Monument
- Lava Butte
- Three Sisters recreation area
- Lava Cast Forest and Lava Lands Visitor Center
- Black Butte
- LaPine State Park
- Sunriver

DOUGLAS COUNTY

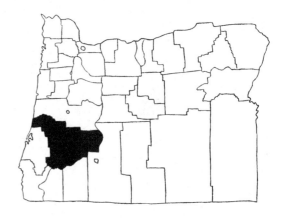

Established	January 7, 1852
County Seat	Roseburg
Population	1970 – 71,743
	1976 – 81,600
	1980 – 93,748
	1990 – 94,649
	2000 – 100,399
Square Miles	5,036
Major Rivers	Umpqua River
Major Mountains	Coast Range, Cascade Range, Umpqua National Forest, Elliott State Forest
Major Lakes	Lemolo Lake, Diamond Lake
Industry	plywood, paper, lumber, metals
Agriculture	fruit
Mining	nickel, gold
Livestock	cattle, hogs, sheep, goats
Logging	Douglas fir, hemlock, western red cedar

Places to Visit

- Diamond Lake
- Umpqua Lighthouse State Park
- Winchester Bay
- Salmon Harbor
- North Umpqua River
- Sulphur Springs near Reedsport
- Douglas County Museum

GILLIAM COUNTY

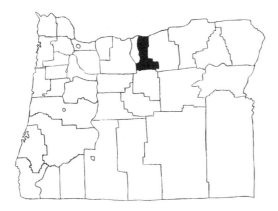

Established	February 25, 1885
County Seat	Condon
Population	1970 – 2,342 1976 – 2,200 1980 – 2,057 1990 – 1,717 2000 – 1,915
Square Miles	1,204
Major Rivers	Columbia River, John Day River, Rock Creek
Major Mountains	Hay Creek Butte, Diamond Butte
Major Lakes	none
Industry	wheat and dry farming
Agriculture	wheat and other grains
Livestock	cattle
Logging	none

Places to Visit

- Condon City Park
- Oregon Trail (7 miles south of Arlington is a sign marking the crossing of the Oregon Trail)
- wheat fields
- hunters of ducks, geese, pheasant, chukar

GRANT COUNTY

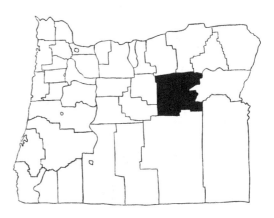

Established	October 14, 1864
County Seat	Canyon City
Population	1970 – 6,996 1976 – 7,430 1980 – 8,210 1990 – 7,853 2000 – 7,935
Square Miles	4,528
Major Rivers	John Day River
Major Mountains	Malheur National Forest, Wallowa-Whitman National Forest, south end of Blue Mountains
Major Lakes	none
Industry	lumber
Agriculture	hay
Livestock	cattle
Logging	ponderosa pine

Places to Visit

- Picture Gorge
- John Day Fossil Beds National Monument
- Joaquin Miller House
- Strawberry Mountain Wilderness
- Kam Wah Chung Historic Site
- John Day Valley
- Long Creek Mountain
- Beech Creek Mountain
- Aldrich Mountain
- Vinegar Hill

HARNEY COUNTY

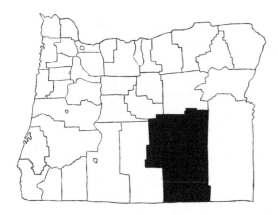

Established	February 25, 1889
County Seat	Burns
Population	1970 – 7,215
	1976 – 7,500
	1980 – 8,314
	1990 – 7,060
	2000 – 7,609
Square Miles	10,134
Major Rivers	Donner and Blitzen Rivers
Major Mountains	Blue Mountains, Steens Mountain, Ochoco National Forest, Malheur National Forest
Major Lakes	Fish Lake, Malheur Lake, Harney Lake, Alvord Lake, Foster Lake
Industry	lumber
Agriculture	hay
Livestock	cattle, sheep
Logging	ponderosa pine

Places to Visit

- Steens Mountain
- Malheur Caves
- Alvord Desert
- Squaw Butte Experimental Station
- Frenchglen Hotel Wayside
- Pete French Round Barn Historic Site
- Warm Springs Butte
- Stinking Water Pass

HOOD RIVER COUNTY

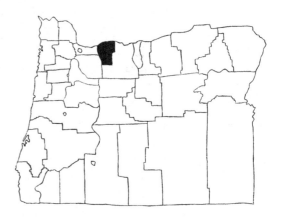

Established	June 23, 1908
County Seat	Hood River
Population	1970 – 13,187
	1976 – 14,450
	1980 – 15,835
	1990 – 16,903
	2000 – 20,411
Square Miles	522
Major Rivers	Hood River, Columbia River, west and east fork of Hood River
Major Mountains	Mount Hood National Forest Mount Hood – 11,240 ft. elevation
Major Lakes	Lost Lake, Wahtum Lake
Industry	lumber, processed foods, textiles
Agriculture	fruits, nuts, berries, pears, apples, cherries
Livestock	dairy cows
Logging	ponderosa pine, Douglas fir, western red cedar

Places to Visit

- Hood River Valley at spring blossom time
- Cascade Locks Marine Park
- Sternwheeler Museum in Cascade Locks
- Bridge of the Gods
- Panorama Point Lava Beds near Parkdale
- Hood River Scenic Railroad to Parkdale
- Barlow Pass
- Wind-surfing on the Columbia River

JACKSON COUNTY

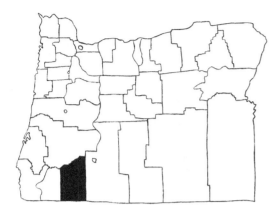

Established	January 12, 1852
County Seat	Medford
Population	1970 – 94,533
	1976 – 113,000
	1980 – 132,456
	1990 – 146,389
	2000 – 181,269
Square Miles	2,785
Major Rivers	Rogue River, Little Butte, Applegate River
Major Mountains	Rogue River National Forest
Major Lakes	Fish Lake
Industry	plywood, lumber, sand, gravel
Agriculture	pears and other fruits
Livestock	cattle and poultry
Logging	Douglas fir and ponderosa pine

Places to Visit

- Jacksonville historical site
- Shakespearean Festival in Ashland
- Southern Oregon State College
- Howard Prairie Reservoir
- Mount Ashland
- Britt Music Festival
- Crater Lake Highway
- Jackson Hot Springs
- Southern Oregon Museum in Jacksonville
- Pear Blossom Festival in Medford
- Beekman Bank in Jacksonville

JEFFERSON COUNTY

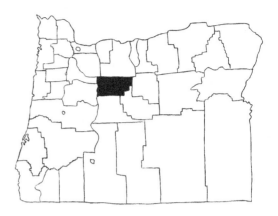

Established	December 12, 1914
County Seat	Madras
Population	1970 – 8,548
	1976 – 9,900
	1980 – 11,599
	1990 – 13,676
	2000 – 19,009
Square Miles	1,780
Major Rivers	Deschutes River, Crooked River, Metolius River
Major Mountains	Willamette National Forest, Mount Jefferson
Major Lakes	Lake Billy Chinook, Lake Simtustus
Industry	lumber and plywood
Agriculture	hay, wheat, clover seeds, potatoes, barley, mint
Livestock	cattle
Logging	pine and Douglas fir

Places to Visit

- Warm Springs Indian Reservation
- Cove Palisades State Park
- Ogden Scenic Wayside
- Springs of the Metolius River
- Black Butte
- Santiam Pass
- Priday Agate Beds
- Kah-Nee-Ta
- Pelton Dam
- Round Butte Dam

JOSEPHINE COUNTY

Established   January 22, 1856

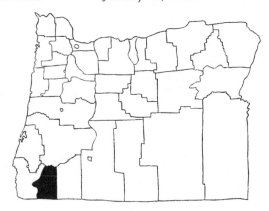

County Seat	Grants Pass
Population	1970 – 35,746
	1976 – 47,000
	1980 – 58,885
	1990 – 62,649
	2000 – 75,726
Square Miles	1,639
Major Rivers	Illinois River, Applegate River, Rogue River
Major Mountains	Siskiyou National Forest, Rogue River National Forest
Major Lakes	Lake Selmac
Industry	lumber, plywood, electrical instruments
Agriculture	vegetables, corn, melons, clover seed
Livestock	cattle, dairy cows
Logging	Douglas fir, ponderosa pine

Places to Visit

- Oregon Caves National Monument
- Rogue River scenic waterway
- Kerbyville Museum
- Wolf Creek Tavern wayside
- Redwood Highway
- Illinois River scenic waterway
- Red Butte Wilderness

KLAMATH COUNTY

Established   October 17, 1882

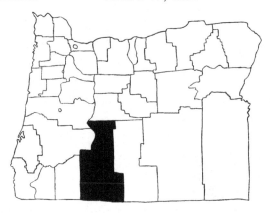

County Seat	Klamath Falls
Population	1970 – 50,021
	1976 – 55,500
	1980 – 59,117
	1990 – 57,702
	2000 – 63,775
Square Miles	5,944
Major Rivers	Link River, Sprague River, Lost River
Major Mountains	Winema National Forest, Rogue River National Forest, Fremont National Forest
Major Lakes	Crescent Lake, Upper Klamath Lake, Crater Lake, Aspen Lake
Industry	lumber and plywood
Agriculture	hay, barley, oats, potatoes, alfalfa
Livestock	cattle
Logging	ponderosa pine, lodgepole pine

Places to Visit

- Crater Lake National Park
- Collier Memorial State Park and Logging Museum
- Lake of the Woods
- Upper Klamath Lake
- Memorial Day Indian Rodeo and Pow-Wow
- Oregon Institute of Technology
- Klamath County Museum
- Favell Museum
- Mount Thielsen Wilderness
- Gearhart Mountain Wilderness

LAKE COUNTY

Established   October 24, 1874

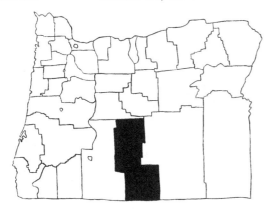

County Seat	Lakeview
Population	1970 – 6,343
	1976 – 6,620
	1980 – 7,532
	1990 – 7,186
	2000 – 7,422
Square Miles	8,135
Major Rivers	Chewaucan River
Major Mountains	Fremont National Forest, Hart Mountain, Deschutes National Forest
Major Lakes	Lake Abert, Summer Lake, Goose Lake, Silver Lake, Hart Lakes, Christmas Lake
Industry	lumber and plywood
Agriculture	hay
Livestock	cattle and sheep
Logging	ponderosa pine and lodgepole pine

Places to Visit

- Hart Mountain National Antelope Refuge
- Old Perpetual Geyser at Hunter's Hot Springs
- Fort Rock State National Area
- Summer Lake Hot Springs
- Abert Land and Rim
- South Ice Cave
- Goose Lake Recreation Area
- Silver Lake
- Schminck Museum in Lakeview

LANE COUNTY

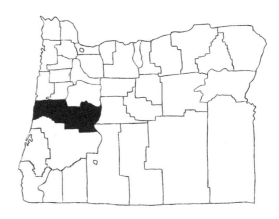

Established	January 28, 1851
County Seat	Eugene
Population	1970 – 213,358
	1976 – 246,000
	1980 – 275,226
	1990 – 282,912
	2000 – 322,959
Square Miles	4,554
Major Rivers	Siuslaw River, McKenzie River, Mohawk River, Long Tom River, Willamette River
Major Mountains	Coast Range, Willamette National Forest, Siuslaw National Forest
Major Lakes	Cougar Lake, Waldo Lake, Fern Ridge Lake
Industry	plywood, paper, lumber, metals, processed foods
Agriculture	vegetables, sweet corn, hay, fruits, nuts, field seeds
Livestock	cattle, poultry, sheep
Logging	Douglas fir, hemlock, spruce, western red cedar

Places to Visit

- Lookout Point Dam and Reservoir, south of Eugene
- Honeyman State Park and sand dunes
- McKenzie River Highway
- University of Oregon in Eugene
- Darlingtonia Botanical Wayside
- Lane County Pioneer Association Museum
- Cougar Dam
- Sea Lion Caves on Coast Highway 101
- Kitson Hot Springs and Belknap Springs
- Cape Perpetua
- Heceta Head Lighthouse

LINCOLN COUNTY

Established   February 20, 1893

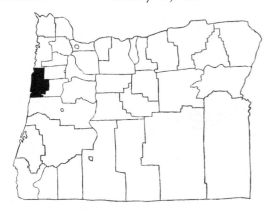

County Seat	Newport
Population	1970 – 25,755
	1976 – 28,100
	1980 – 35,264
	1990 –38,889
	2000 – 44,479
Square Miles	979
Major Rivers	Yaquina River, Alsea River, Siletz River
Major Mountains	Siuslaw National Forest
Major Lakes	Devil's Lake
Industry	paper and processed foods
Agriculture	hay, forest product specialties, plywood, shingles
Livestock	dairy cows
Logging	Douglas fir, hemlock, western redcedar, spruce

Places to Visit

- Boiler Bay State Park
- Otter Crest Viewpoint
- Yaquina Bay Lighthouse
- OSU Marine Science Center
- Agate Beach
- Devil's Punchbowl State Park
- Road's End in Lincoln City
- Cape Perpetua
- Depoe Bay
- Cape Foulweather
- Newport Marina

LINN COUNTY

Established   December 28, 1847

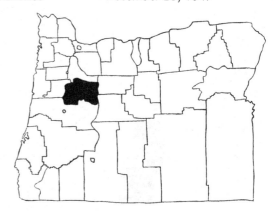

County Seat	Albany
Population	1970 – 71,914
	1976 – 83,400
	1980 – 89,495
	1990 – 91,227
	2000 – 103,069
Square Miles	2,292
Major Rivers	Willamette River, Calapooya River, South Santiam River, McKenzie River
Major Mountains	Cascade Range, Willamette National Forest, Santiam State Forest
Major Lakes	Detroit Lake, Clear Lake, Big Lake
Industry	plywood, lumber, metals
Agriculture	field seeds, hay, vegetables, sweet corn
Livestock	cattle, sheep, poultry, dairy cows
Logging	Douglas fir, hemlock, western red cedar

Places to Visit

- Cascadia State Park
- Brownsville Historical Museum
- Carmen Reservoir
- Timber Carnival on July 4th in Albany
- Detroit Lake State Park
- Mount Jefferson Wilderness
- Clear Lake
- Koosah Falls
- Hoodoo Ski Bowl
- Mount Washington wilderness

MALHEUR COUNTY

Established   February 17, 1887

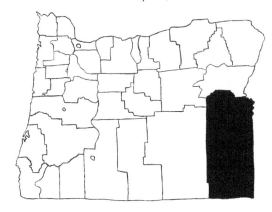

County Seat	Vale
Population	1970 – 23,169
	1976 – 24,600
	1980 – 26,896
	1990 – 26,038
	2000 – 31,615
Square Miles	9,887
Major Rivers	Owyhee River Scenic Waterway, Malheur River
Major Mountains	Sheepshead Mountains, Mahogany Mountains
Major Lakes	Owyhee Lake, Cow Lakes, Coyote Lake
Industry	processed foods
Agriculture	sugar beets, potatoes, vegetables, hay, alfalfa
Livestock	cattle, dairy cows, sheep
Logging	none

Places to Visit

- Owyhee Lake
- Jordan Valley
- Basque settlements
- Snake River
- Beulah Reservoir
- Turnbull Lake Bed
- Oregon Trail Interpretive Site (on Interstate 84 northwest of Ontario)
- Watchable Wildlife Interpretive Site
- Lava beds in western side of county
- Rockhound areas

MARION COUNTY

Established   July 5, 1843

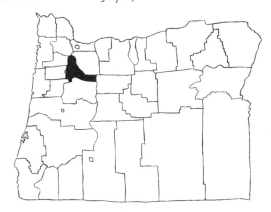

County Seat	Salem
Population	1970 – 151,309
	1976 – 173.300
	1980 – 204,692
	1990 – 228,483
	2000 –284,834
Square Miles	1,183
Major Rivers	Willamette River, North Santiam River, Breitenbush River
Major Mountains	Mount Hood National Forest
Major Lakes	Elk Lake
Industry	plywood, paper, processed foods, metals
Agriculture	vegetables, sweet corn, fruits, nuts, berries, grass seed
Livestock	sheep, hogs, poultry, dairy cows
Logging	none

Places to Visit

- State capitol building in Salem
- Champoeg State Park
- Silver Creek Falls
- Silver Falls State Park
- Detroit Dam
- French Prairie
- Aurora
- Mount Angel Abby
- Willamette University
- Breitenbush Hot Springs

MORROW COUNTY

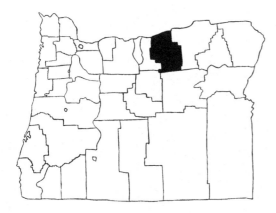

Established	February 16, 1885
County Seat	Heppner
Population	1970 – 4,465
	1976 – 5,350
	1980 – 7,519
	1990 – 7,625
	2000 – 10,995
Square Miles	2,032
Major Rivers	Columbia River, Willow Creek
Major Mountains	Umatilla National Forest, Black Mountain, Madison Butte
Industry	farming
Agriculture	wheat, hay, barley
Livestock	cattle
Logging	none

Places to Visit

- Columbia River
- Fossil beds near Boardman
- Umatilla National Forest
- Route of the Oregon Trail near Cecil
- Umatilla National Wildlife Refuge

MULTNOMAH COUNTY

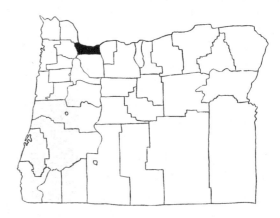

Established	December 2, 1854
County Seat	Portland
Population	1970 – 554,668
	1976 – 553,000
	1980 – 562,640
	1990 – 583,887
	2000 – 660,486
Square Miles	435
Major Rivers	Columbia River, Willamette River, Sandy River
Major Mountains	Mount Hood National Forest
Major Lakes	Blue Lake
Industry	plywood, paper, machinery, metals, textiles
Agriculture	nursery and greenhouse plants, berries, vegetables, sweet corn, nuts
Livestock	poultry, dairy cows
Logging	Douglas fir and hemlock

Places to Visit

- Portland Art Museum
- Rose Garden
- The Grotto
- Oregon Zoo
- OMSI
- Lloyd Center
- Larch Mountain
- Multnomah Falls
- Columbia River Gorge Scenic Drive
- Pittock Mansion
- Old Columbia Highway
- Bridal Veil Falls
- Horsetail Falls
- World Forestry Center Museum

POLK COUNTY

Established   December 22, 1845

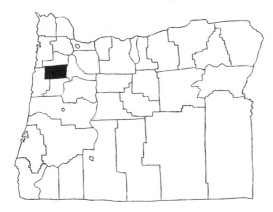

County Seat	Dallas
Population	1970 – 35,349
	1976 – 41,400
	1980 – 45,203
	1990 – 49,541
	2000 – 62,380
Square Miles	741
Major Rivers	Willamette River, Luckiamute River, Siletz River
Major Mountains	Coast Range
Major Lakes	Valsetz Lake
Industry	lumber, plywood, machinery
Agriculture	cherries, plums, prunes, nuts, grains, field seeds, mint, vegetables
Livestock	dairy cows, sheep, poultry
Logging	Douglas fir and hemlock

Places to Visit

- Buena Vista River Ferry
- Western Oregon State College
- Rickreall Creek
- Helmick State Park
- Ritner Creek covered bridge on State Route # 223

SHERMAN COUNTY

Established   February 25, 1889

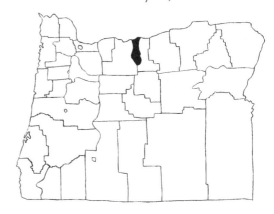

County Seat	Moro
Population	1970 – 2,139
	1976 – 2,190
	1980 – 2,172
	1990 – 1,918
	2000 – 1,934
Square Miles	823
Major Rivers	Deschutes River, Columbia River, John Day River
Major Mountains	none
Major Lakes	none
Industry	farming
Agriculture	wheat, barley, oats
Livestock	cattle
Logging	none

Places to Visit

- John Day River scenic waterway
- John Day Dam near Rufus
- Deschutes River scenic waterway
- Columbia River
- Deschutes River Recreation Area

TILLAMOOK COUNTY

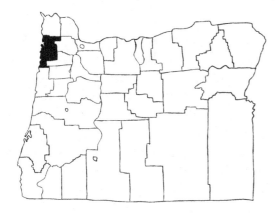

Established	December 15, 1853
County Seat	Tillamook
Population	1970 – 18,034
	1976 – 18,600
	1980 – 21,164
	1990 – 21,570
	2000 – 24,262
Square Miles	1,102
Major Rivers	Wilson River, Tillamook River, Trask River, Nestucca River, Nehalem River, Miami River
Major Mountains	Coast Range, Tillamook State Forest
Major Lakes	none
Industry	dairy products, lumber, processed foods
Agriculture	forestry
Livestock	dairy cows
Logging	Douglas fir, hemlock, spruce

Places to Visit

- Three Arch Rocks National Wildlife Refuge
- Octopus Tree at Cape Meares
- Neahkahnie Mountain
- Cascade Head
- Cape Lookout State Park
- Cape Meares Lighthouse
- Oswald West State Park
- Cape Kiwanda State Park
- Tillamook Bay

UMATILLA COUNTY

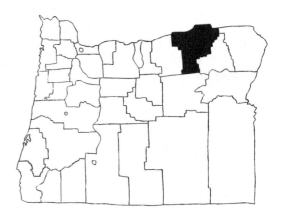

Established	September 27, 1862
County Seat	Pendleton
Population	1970 – 44,923
	1976 – 50,000
	1980 – 58,861
	1990 – 59,249
	2000 – 70,548
Square Miles	3,215
Major Rivers	Umatilla River, Columbia River
Major Mountains	Blue Mountains, Umatilla National Forest
Major Lakes	McKay Creek Reservoir
Industry	lumber, furniture, processed foods, textiles
Agriculture	wheat, barley, vegetables, hay, peas, potatoes
Livestock	cattle, sheep, hogs
Logging	Douglas fir, ponderosa pine

Places to Visit

- McNary Dam
- Pendleton Roundup
- Battle Mountain State Park
- Hat Rock State Park
- Oregon Trail Interpretive Site southwest of Echo
- Emigrant Springs State Park
- Lehman Hot Springs
- Cold Springs National Wildlife Refuge
- McKay Creek Wildlife Refuge
- Blue Mountain Forest wayside

UNION COUNTY

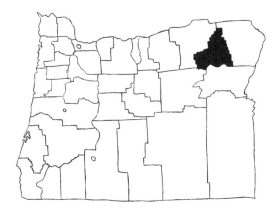

Established	October 14, 1864
County Seat	La Grande
Population	1970 – 19,377
	1976 – 22,200
	1980 – 23,921
	1990 – 23,598
	2000 – 24,530
Square Miles	2,036
Major Rivers	Grande Ronde River
Major Mountains	Blue Mountains, Wallowa Mountains, Umatilla National Forest, Wallowa-Whitman National Forest
Major Lakes	Anthony Lakes, Olive Lake
Industry	lumber, plywood, machinery, farming
Agriculture	wheat, hay, fruit, grass seed
Livestock	cattle, hogs
Logging	Douglas fir, ponderosa pine, lodgepole pine

Places to Visit

- Grande Ronde Valley
- Spout Springs
- Eastern Oregon College
- Meacham winter area
- Tollgate winter area
- Blue Mountain Rodeo
- Cove Hot Springs
- Catherine Creek State Park
- Oregon Trail Interpretive Park
- Red Bridge wayside
- Eastern Oregon Timber Carnival

WALLOWA COUNTY

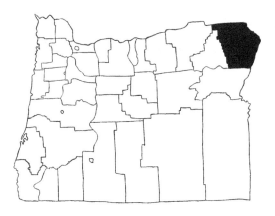

Established	February 11, 1887
County Seat	Enterprise
Population	1970 – 6,247
	1976 – 6,880
	1980 – 7,273
	1990 – 6,911
	2000 – 7,226
Square Miles	3,145
Major Rivers	Wallowa River, Grande Ronde River, Minam River
Major Mountains	Matterhorn Mountain, Wallowa-Whitman National Forest, Umatilla National Forest
Major Lakes	Wallowa Lake, Minam Lake
Industry	lumber
Agriculture	wheat, hay
Livestock	cattle
Logging	Douglas fir, ponderosa pine

Places to Visit

- Wallowa Lake State Park
- Minam State Recreation Area
- Eagle Cap Wilderness
- Hells Canyon National Recreation Area
- Wallowa National Forest
- Hurricane Creek Canyon
- Mount Howard

WASCO COUNTY

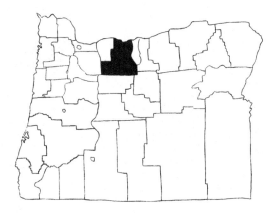

Established	January 11, 1854
County Seat	The Dalles
Population	1970 – 20,133
	1976 – 20,300
	1980 – 21,732
	1990 – 21,683
	2000 – 23,791
Square Miles	2,381
Major Rivers	Columbia River, Deschutes River
Major Mountains	Mount Hood National Forest
Major Lakes	Twin Lakes
Industry	lumber, metals, electric power
Agriculture	wheat, barley, cherries
Livestock	cattle, sheep
Logging	Douglas fir, ponderosa pine

Places to Visit

- The Dalles Dam
- Sorosis Park and Viewpoint
- Columbia River Gorge scenic area
- Deschutes River Scenic waterway
- Heritage Landing State Park
- Badger Creek Wilderness
- White River Falls State Park
- Oregon Trail at Tygh Valley near Dufur
- Pulpit Rock
- Fort Dalles Museum
- Old Wasco County Courthouse
- Wasco County Historical Museum

WASHINGTON COUNTY

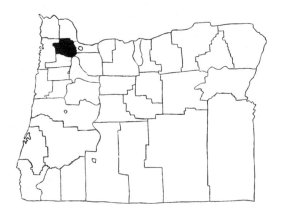

Established	July 5, 1843
County Seat	Hillsboro
Population	1970 – 157,920
	1976 – 196,000
	1980 – 247,800
	1990 – 311,554
	2000 – 445,342
Square Miles	723
Major Rivers	Tualatin River
Major Mountains	Coast Range, Tillamook State Forest
Major Lakes	Hagg Lake
Industry	plywood, electrical instruments, machinery
Agriculture	plums, prunes, hazelnuts (filberts), walnuts, nursery plants, grains, vegetables, hay
Livestock	dairy cows
Logging	Douglas fir, western hemlock

Places to Visit

- Wilson River
- Sunset Highway
- Tualatin Valley Orchards
- Pacific University in Forest Grove
- Old Scotch Church north of Hillsboro
- Gales Creek area
- Alpenrose Dairyland

WHEELER COUNTY

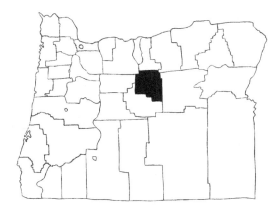

Established   February 17, 1899

County Seat   Fossil

Population   1970 – 1,849
                     1976 – 2,030
                     1980 – 1,513
                     1990 – 1,396
                     2000 – 1,547

Square Miles   1,714

Major Rivers   John Day River

Major Mountains Ochoco National Forest

Major Lakes   Rock Creek Lake

Industry   lumber

Agriculture   none

Livestock   cattle, sheep

Logging   ponderosa pine, Douglas fir

Places to Visit

- John Day River
- John Day Fossil Beds National Monument
- Painted Hills State Park
- Shelton State Park
- Black Canyon Wilderness
- Bridge Creek Wilderness
- Clarno State Park
- Squaw Butte
- Baldy Mountain

YAMHILL COUNTY

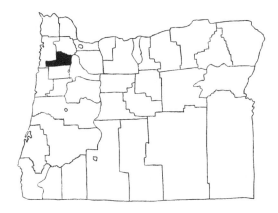

Established   July 5, 1843

County Seat   McMinnville

Population   1970 – 40,213
                     1976 – 45,700
                     1980 – 55,332
                     1990 – 65,551
                     2000 – 84,992

Square Miles   715

Major Rivers   North Yamhill River, South Yamhill River, Willamette River

Major Mountains Coast Range, Siuslaw National Forest

Major Lakes   Carlton Lake, Meadow Lake

Industry   paper, mobile homes, plywood, lumber

Agriculture   plums, prunes, hazelnuts (filberts), walnuts, hay, vegetables, grains

Livestock   dairy cows, poultry, sheep

Logging   none

Places to Visit

- Yamhill County Historical Museum
- Herbert Hoover House in Newberg
- George Fox College in Newberg
- Linfield College in McMinnville
- Historic Dayton
- Yamhill Locks County Park
- Maud Williams State Park
- Bald Peak State Park

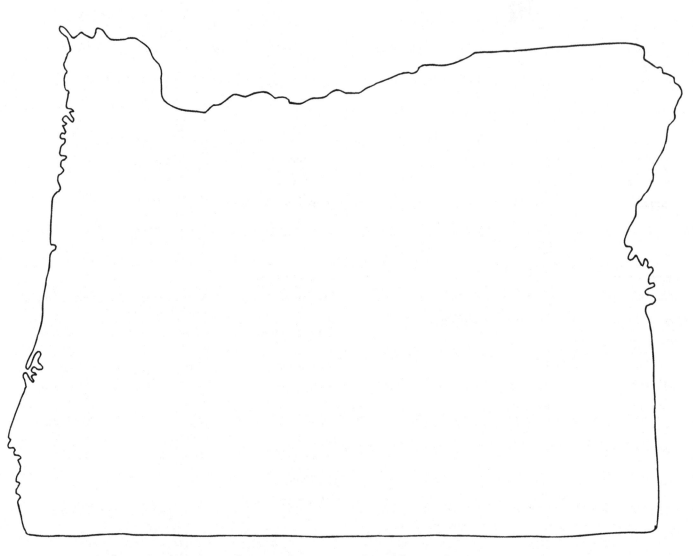

Using an atlas or roadmap, place ten major cities and your
home town on the map above.

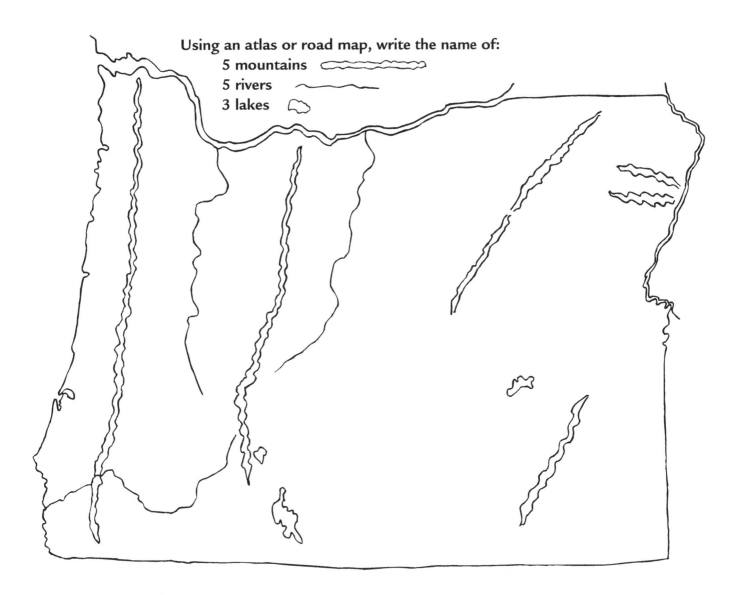

Using an atlas or road map, write the name of:
5 mountains
5 rivers
3 lakes

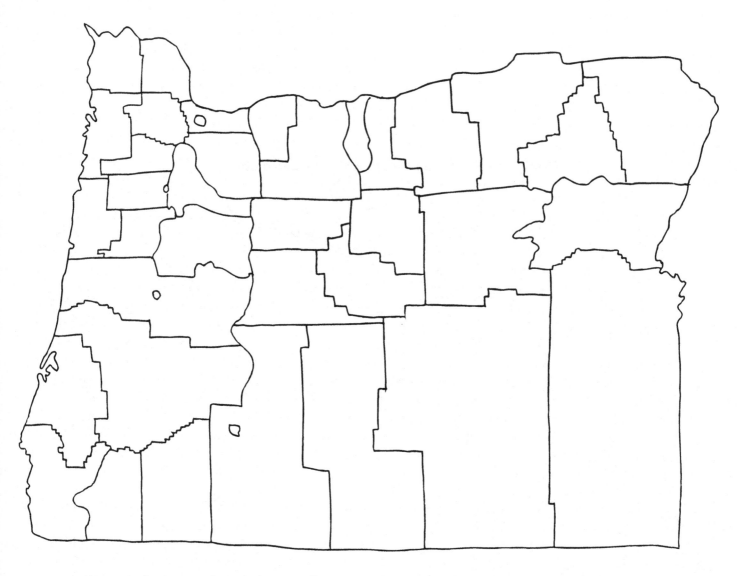

Using an atlas or road map, locate all 36 counties. Write the names of the counties in the proper place.

CITIES OF OREGON

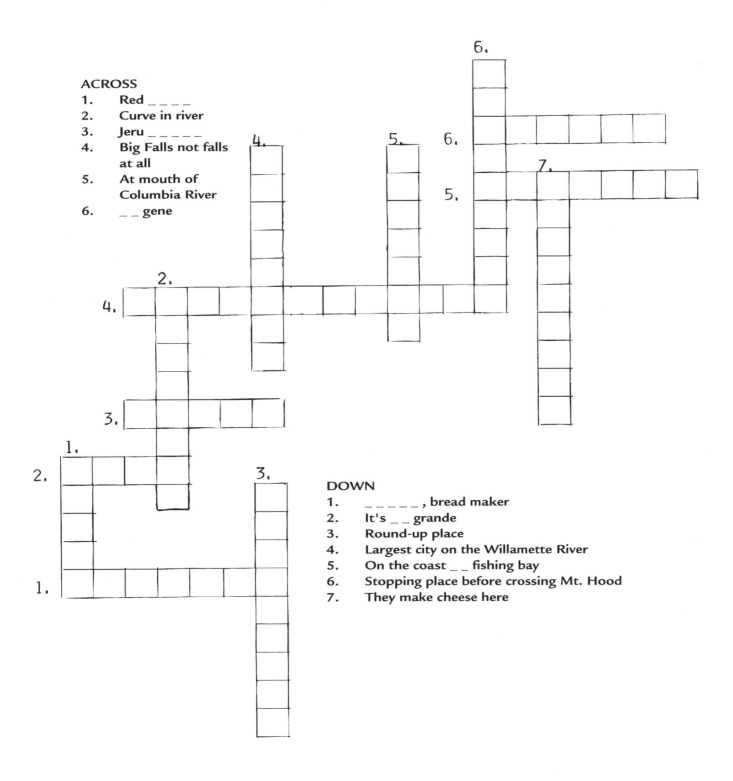

ACROSS
1. Red _ _ _ _
2. Curve in river
3. Jeru _ _ _ _ _
4. Big Falls not falls at all
5. At mouth of Columbia River
6. _ _ gene

DOWN
1. _ _ _ _ _ , bread maker
2. It's _ _ grande
3. Round-up place
4. Largest city on the Willamette River
5. On the coast _ _ fishing bay
6. Stopping place before crossing Mt. Hood
7. They make cheese here

149

**NOW GO BACK AND STUDY ALL THE QUESTIONS
FOR UNIT VIII TO PREPARE FOR THE FINAL TEST.**

Suggested Projects

1. Using your road map of Oregon, use a black pen and outline each of the 36 counties.

2. Find the county you live in. Write down as many places to visit in your county as you can.

3. Go to your local library and find who your local town mayor is? Who is the county commissioner? Is there a county treasurer? Who is the county sheriff? Can you visit the sheriff's office?
    The county courthouse? Who is the judge?

4. Using your state map, plan a family vacation. Be sure to get your parents' permission. Maybe they would help you plan the trip with you. Now take a red pen and show the route you will take.

5. Go to a local travel bureau or agency and get some free brochures showing the places you would like to visit. Using the Oregon road map and the brochures, make that planned vacation a show-and-tell time.

Bibliography

Atlas of the Pacific Northwest Resources and Development, ed., by Richard M. Highsmith Jr., Corvallis: Oregon State University Press, 1968.

Babcock, Chester, and Babcock, Clare Applegate, *Our Pacific Northwest Yesterday and Today,* St. Louis: McGraw-Hill Book Co., Inc., 1963.

Bakeless, John, *The Journals of Lewis and Clark,* New York: The New American Library, A Mentor Book, 1964.

Bedingfield, Nancy, *Oregon's 100 Years in Pictures,* Portland, Oregon: Binfords & Mort, 1958.

Berry, Don, *A Majority of Scoundrels,* Sausalito, California: A Comstock Edition, 1961.

Bingham, Edwin, *Oregon!,* Santa Barbara: Peregrine Smith, Inc., 1979.

Boyle, Donzella Cross, *Quest of a Hemisphere,* Massachusetts: Western Islands, 1970.

Case, Robert Ormond, *River of the West, A Story of Opportunity in the Columbia Empire,* Portland, Oregon: Northwestern Electric Co., Pacific Power and Light Co., 1940.

Coffman, Lloyd W., *Blazing a Wagon Trail to Oregon,* Springfield, Oregon: Echo Books, 1993.

Culp, Edwin D., *Oregon the Way It Was,* Caxton Printers, Ltd., Caldwell, Idaho: 1983.

Daugherty, James, *Marcus and Narcissa Whitman, Pioneers of Oregon,* New York: The Viking Press, 1953.

Dicken, Samuel N., and Dicken, Emily F., *The Making of Oregon, A Study in Historical Geography,* Portland, Oregon: Oregon Historical Society, 1979.

Douthit, Mary Osborn, *The Souvenir of Western Women,* Portland, Oregon: Anderson & Duniway Co., 1905.

Duncan, Dayton and Burns, Ken, *Lewis and Clark, The Journey of the Corps of Discovery,* Alfred A. Knopf, New York: 1997.

Down, Robert H., *Oregon's Century of Education,* Information from the Oregon Historical Society, Portland, Oregon: 1977.

Fadeley, Nancie Peacocke, *Mission To Oregon,* Eugene, Oregon: 1976.

Friedman, Ralph, *This Side of Oregon,* Caldwell, Idaho: The Caxton Printers, Ltd., 1983.

Friedman, Ralph, *Oregon for the Curious,* Portland, Oregon: Pars Publishing Co., 1965.

Friedman, Ralph, *Oregon for the Curious,* Caldwell, Idaho: The Caxton Printers, Ltd., 1982.

Friedman, Ralph, *Tracking Down Oregon,* Caldwell, Idaho: The Caxton Printers, Ltd., 1978.

Gilbert, Bill, and the editors of Time-Life Books, *The Old West, The Trailblazers,* New York: Time-Life Books, 1973.

Gish, Duane T., Ph.D., *Evolution, The Fossils Say No!,* Creation Life Pub., San Diego: 1973.

"Indian, American," *The World Book Encyclopedia,* 1972 ed., Vol. 10, pp. 108-139.

"Indian Wars," *The World Book Encyclopedia,* 1972 ed., Vol. 10, pp. 144-149.

Johansen, Dorothy O., *Empire On The Columbia,* New York: Harper & Row, 1967.

Junell, Joseph S., *Exploring The Northwest,* Chicago: Fallet Publishing Co., 1966.

Lampman, Linda and Sterling, Julie, *The Portland Guidebook,* Mercer Island: The Writing Words, Inc., 1978.

Lockley, Fred, *Visionaries, Mountain Men & Empire Builders,* Eugene, Oregon: Rainy Day Press, 1982.

Maddux, Percy, *City On the Willamette,* Portland, Oregon: Binfords & Mort., 1952.

Maehle and Mitchell, *Let's Tour the Pacific Northwest,* St. Louis: Milliken Pub. Co., 1969.

McKay, Daring Donald, *The Lost War Trail of the Modocs,* ed. by Keith and Donna Clark, Oregon Historical Society, Portland, Oregon: 1971.

Meacham, Walter, *Barlow Road,* Oregon Council, American Pioneer Trails Association, 1947.

Morris, Henry M. and Parker, Gary E., *What is Creation Science?,* Master Books, El Cajon: 1982.

O'Brien, Mary Barmeyer, *Heart of the Trail,* Helena: Falcon Pub., Inc., 1997.

Olson, Joan and Olson, Gene, *Washington Times and Trails,* Rogue River, Oregon: Windyridge Press, 1970.

Olson, Joan and Olson, Gene, *Oregon Times and Trails,* Grants Pass, Oregon: Windyridge Press, 1972.

"Oregon," *The World Book Encyclopedia,* 1972 ed., Vol. 14, pp. 626-643.

Our Indian Friends, Salem, Oregon: Salem Public Schools, 1961.

Powell, James Madison, M.D., *"Powell History,"* 1922.

Reader's Digest, *American Fascinating Indian Heritage,* Pleasantville, New York, The Reader's Digest Association, Inc., 1978.

Reader's Digest, Ed., Calkins, Carroll, *"The Story of America,"* The Reader's Digest Association, 1975, pp. 68-85, pp.158-171, pp. 190-207.

Richardson, Ruth E., *Oregon History Stories,* Valley Printing Co.,Eugene, Oregon: 1938.

Schlissel, Lillian, *Women's Diaries of the Westward Journey,* New York: Schocken Books, 1982.

Scofield, William E., *Northwest Heritage,* New York: Amsca School Pub., Inc., 1978.

Smith, Ronald O., and Falkenstein, Lynda, *Rendezvous in the Pacific Northwest,* Portland, Oregon: Great Western Pub. Co., 1979.

Smith-Western Inc., Publisher, *Scenic Oregon,* Portland, Oregon: Dexter Press.

Snyder, Gerald S., *In the Footsteps of Lewis and Clark,* National Geographic Society, 1970.

Sunset Travel Guide to Oregon, editors of Sunset Books, Menlo Park: Lane Pub. Co., 1976.

Taylor, Arthur S., Stone, Buena Cobb, Foster, Irene, *Our Great Northwest,* San Francisco: Harr Wagner Pub. Co., 1854.

The Editors of America West, *The Great Northwest, The Story of a Land and Its People,* New York: Weathervane Books, 1973.

The National Historical Society, *The Lewis and Clark Expedition,* Gettysburg: 1970.

The Oregon Story, Salem, Oregon: Salem Public Schools, Centennial Ed., 1959.

The Oregon Story, Salem, Oregon: Salem Public Schools, 1968.

Tiner, John Hudson, *When Science Fails,* Baker Book House, Grand Rapids:1974.

United States Department of the Interior, *Multi-Purpose Dams of the Pacific Northwest,* Bonneville Power Administration.

Ward, Geoffrey C., *The West "An Illustrated History,"* Little, Brown and Co., 1996.

"Washington," The World Book Encyclopedia, 1972 ed., Vol. 21, pp. 46 -61.

"Western Movement," The World Book Encyclopedia, 1972 ed., Vol. 21, pp. 200-211.

Western On the Oregon Trail, New York: American Heritage Pub. Co., Inc., 1962.

Made in the USA
Coppell, TX
03 July 2020